A CHAMPION'S GUIDE TO SUCCESS IN SPELLING BEES

Fundamentals of Spelling Bee Competition and Preparation

NED G. ANDREWS
1994 Scripps National Spelling Bee Champion

CreateSpace
Charleston, South Carolina

Library of Congress Cataloging-in-Publication Data

Andrews, Ned G.
A champion's guide to success in spelling bees : fundamentals of spelling bee competition and preparation / Ned G. Andrews.

First edition, tenth printing
p. cm.

ISBN-13: 978-1463689087
ISBN-10: 146368908X

Library classification information applied for and pending:
1. Library of Congress Subject Heading(s)
2. Call numbers:
    a. Library of Congress Classification
    b. Dewey Decimal Classification

Library of Congress Control Number: 2011912010

Front cover image (now in public domain):
Illustrator: Francesco Stelluti
Engraver: Matthaeus Greuter
Source: *PERSIO* [Aulus Persius Flaccus] *tradotto in verso sciolto e dichiarato* (Francesco Stelluti, translator), Rome: Giacomo Mascardi, 1630, page 52.

Photograph on back cover (used with permission):
William H. Andrews Jr.

Printed in the United States of America
CreateSpace · Charleston, South Carolina

TABLE OF CONTENTS

ACKNOWLEDGMENTS

First, a salute to history: Noah Webster, more than any single other person, was responsible for establishing American spelling as a unique institution. In addition, he made the first concerted effort toward introducing the science of etymology into the art of lexicography, making possible the question-and-answer format that adds so much to the educational value of competitive spelling. The E. W. Scripps Company brought competitive spelling to the national prominence it enjoys today.

The E. W. Scripps Company, the Scripps and non-Scripps newspapers that sponsor local spelling bees and national-level contestants, and other companies have provided student competitors with innumerable rewards and incentives. In particular, I send personal thanks to the *Knoxville News Sentinel* (styled the *Knoxville News–Sentinel* during my time in competition) for its sponsorship of my five regional competitions and three trips to the Scripps National Spelling Bee finals.

James Maguire lent his experienced eye to this guide by reviewing and commenting on its initial draft; he also provided guidelines and suggestions on which I relied heavily when selecting its final title. George Thampy, the SNSB's 2000 national champion, reviewed and commented on the draft from the perspective of a successful competitor, as well as catching what I must confess to have been the occasional typographical error. In addition to his personal and academic guidance over the years, Jeff Brenzel provided me with advice about the publication process.

Melodee Baines' love inspired me to see this project through, and her tenacity in her own scholarship continues to stand as both an example and a challenge.

Finally, without the constant support of Carolyn Andrews, my mother and spelling coach, to whom this guide is dedicated, I likely would never have learned the fundamentals of spelling bee competition and preparation.

PREFACE

This guidebook's primary purpose is to help its readers develop the skills that spelling bees demand and make the most of the skills that they have developed so far. It doubles as a guide for spelling coaches or tutors – usually educators, former competitors, or other "verbivores," to use Richard Lederer's term – who have been enlisted to help prospective competitors. Finally, it will be of interest to people who have no plans to compete but who wonder why others choose to compete and what it takes to succeed.

Readers may note that when viewed chronologically from the perspective of someone serious about competitive spelling, this guide is "written backward": It discusses what to do during competition before it discusses what skills you need to develop if you're to compete successfully, and it discusses how someone with well-developed spelling skills will use them before it discusses how to develop them in the first place.

From a conceptual perspective, however, reverse chronological order is best for discussing what it takes to succeed at competitive spelling. To make sense of what you're doing when you use the study methods that this guide suggests, it helps to know *why* you're doing what you're doing – that is, to have a clear understanding of what types of information you will learn and what specific skills you will develop as you study. Likewise, any discussion of when and why a given skill is useful will make a lot more sense if you're familiar with the various ways in which the competition's rules enable you to apply your overall set of skills.

In addition, discussing competition first is more efficient: If you have only short notice of an upcoming competition and don't have much time to prepare, **you can gain a lot by reading just the first chapter and applying its techniques**

1

to information that you already know – even if you don't take time to learn any additional words, word elements, spelling rules, or spelling patterns.

Readers may also note what *isn't* in this guide: It does not contain lists of "good spelling bee words," foreign word elements that occur frequently in competition, spelling rules for English, or spelling rules or transliteration conventions for other languages that have "lent" words to English. Lists of such words and elements amount to collections of raw data, and the rules and conventions in question represent highly context-sensitive patterns followed by certain subsets (most notably, groups of words sharing a language of origin) of that data set. It can take years of preparation to become familiar enough with these data and patterns that you stand a good chance of advancing to high levels of competition, and it's impossible (at least as a practical matter) to list every single one of them.

Instead, this guide will give you important advice about where to find these words and elements and about how to figure out these rules and conventions. Perhaps more importantly, it will give you time- and field-tested guidance about how to learn all that you can from this information, including ways of collecting and organizing it that will help you develop intuitions beyond the mere explicit recognition of particular patterns. In other words, **this guide is not a "study book" in the usual sense of the term — it's the book that you need to read *before* you spend time with study books, word lists, dictionaries, and other sources of specific pieces of information.**

Two notes on abbreviations:

1. "SNSB" or "[t]he SNSB" refers to the Scripps National Spelling Bee, the United States of America's premier

spelling competition for elementary and middle or junior high school students.

2. *"Webster's Third"* refers to the latest edition of *Webster's Third New International Dictionary*, published by Merriam-Webster, Inc. *Webster's Third* is the official dictionary of the SNSB, and the SNSB recommends that its contestants' sponsors use *Webster's Third* in their regional and local competitions.[1]

I would finish this introduction by wishing you luck, but contrary to popular opinion, the luck that you have during competition isn't all that important. (I'll have some thoughts on that point at the end of this guide.) Instead, let's jump to the competition itself: how to get and use every available piece of information about a word with which you're faced.

---

[1] *Webster's Fourth New International Dictionary* is currently under development. When it is published, it will become the official dictionary of the SNSB and the dictionary that the SNSB recommends that its contestants' sponsors use. *See* Barrie Trinkle, Carolyn Andrews, and Paige Kimble, *How to Spell Like a Champ: Roots, Lists, Rules, Games, Tricks, & Bee-Winning Tips from the Pros* (New York: Workman Publishing, 2006, ISBN-13 #978-0-7611-4369-7), page 32. (Disclosure: I am acknowledged on page viii and quoted on pages 44 and 160 of this book.) For more information on Carolyn Andrews, see note 19 below.

CHAPTER I:
COMPETITION

If you're reading this guidebook to begin with, then you're in all likelihood familiar with the traditional format of spelling bees: Each competitor is given a word to spell and is allowed to ask certain questions about that word. The competitor then spells the word and, with certain exceptions during the final rounds of competition, either advances or is eliminated.

The questions that you're allowed to ask are a crucial source of information about the word that you've been given. The pronouncer's responses will give you clues – or sometimes outright answers – as to what your word's elements or roots are and what patterns its spelling likely follows. If you think that you know your word, the answers that you get will help you make sure that you have the right word in mind. Even if you are unfamiliar with your word, those answers will help make your guess about its spelling as educated as possible.

For these reasons, **success in competition begins with making sure you know what questions you're allowed to ask, when you should ask them, and what you should do with the information that you get.**

1: THE QUESTIONS
WHAT THEY ARE AND WHAT THEY DO FOR YOU

Most spelling bees allow you to ask the pronouncer or the judges for some or all of the following information:

1. **Repronunciation** of your word
   a. Whether a **test pronunciation** that you propose for your word is correct
   b. Any **alternate pronunciations** that your word may have

2. Your word's **definition**
    a. Any **alternate definitions** that your word may have
3. Your word's **language of origin**
4. Confirmation of **whether your word descends from a specific English or foreign root** that you provide
5. An example of your word's **use in a sentence**

Some bees, particularly classroom and school bees that might not use unabridged dictionaries, will not let you ask all of these questions. In 2007, the SNSB began recommending that local bees not entertain questions about specific root words or alternate definitions.[2] It is my guess that the SNSB's national officials discourage these questions at local levels because they worry that local officials will be unable to answer them properly (for example, because of a lack of familiarity with unabridged dictionaries).

However, it is good to be familiar with all of these questions for three reasons.

1. Many local and regional competitions *are* equipped to handle these questions, and some honor them. The closer you get to national competition, the more similar to it your current bee will likely be (with the exception of the time limits in place at nationals), and the more likely it is that you will be allowed to ask a given question and benefit from the information that its answer reveals.

2. As of this guide's publication, all of these questions except a request for alternate definitions are allowed in national

---

[2] See, for example, "Speller's requests" in Rule 5 of the SNSB's 2010 "Rules for Local Spelling Bees," available via the Internet Archive at http://web.archive.org/web/20120915064145/http://www.spellingbee. com/files / spellingbee. com / Rules %20 for %20 Local %20 Spelling %20 Bees.pdf (requires Adobe/Acrobat Reader; "%20" represents a space and can be replaced with one in some browsers).

competition, and to be successful at nationals you must know how to use all of the questions to which you are entitled.

3. To be fully familiar with these questions by "Bee Week" (the week during which nationals are held), you need to begin learning how to use them even before you qualify. The earlier you learn how to use them, the more you can practice and the better you will be at using them if and when the time comes.

The following are the ways in which each question can help you figure out how to spell your word.

1. **Repronunciation:**

Asking for a repronunciation, *i.e.*, asking the pronouncer to repeat the first listed pronunciation of your word, serves two purposes, each of which is important but limited.

a) If you believe that the pronouncer has given you some specific word, a repronunciation can help confirm whether that word is in fact the word that the pronouncer gave you. If you hear the same sounds the second time and if the sounds that you've heard each time match the pronunciation of the word that you have in mind, chances are that the word that you have in mind is the one that you are being asked to spell. (But beware: You may have had the same trouble hearing each time you heard the word.)

b) If you did not clearly hear all or part of the word when the pronouncer first said it for you, a repronunciation can help fill in the gap or gaps. Once you have heard the complete sequence of sounds, you can start figuring out how to spell the word that those sounds represent.

Test pronunciation:

As an alternative to asking for a repronunciation, you may confirm what you believe to be the correct pronunciation by repeating that pronunciation for the judges and observing whether they approve of it as being correct. (The judges at nationals encourage this practice.)

Offering a test pronunciation is especially useful immediately before you spell your word. In addition to reconfirming what word it is, saying your word one last time brings it to the forefront of your mind and helps you visualize it as you spell.

- Be careful, though, not to "overpronounce" (*i.e.*, to give disproportionate emphasis or articulation to one or more sounds within your word), especially in the case of schwas. Doing so amounts to asking the pronouncer to approve of a mispronunciation and is improper for additional reasons that I discuss below.

Alternate pronunciations:

In most bees, you may ask for any additional ("alternate") pronunciations that a word might have. Asking for alternate pronunciations may come in very handy if you are attempting to "sound out" a word or part of a word. For example, suppose that you hear a pronunciation in which a schwa is pronounced "dotted" (higher in the mouth than completely neutral position) or a consonant is devoiced (pronounced with the vocal cords stopped, as for *t* as opposed to *d*). You will know that the word can be spelled only with letters that can be pronounced in the ways that you hear. Then you can rule out spellings that use other letters that do not fit the alternate pronunciation.

- *Especially if you have already asked for alternate pronunciations, do NOT ask whether a word can be pronounced in a particular way that you have not yet heard.*

It is acceptable to confirm an alternate pronunciation by repeating it to the pronouncer. In local competition, it is acceptable in extreme cases to ask whether you have been given all the pronunciations listed in the dictionary. (At nationals, it is standard practice to give all listed pronunciations when a speller asks for alternate pronunciations.) However, that is as far as you should go.

Trying to put sounds into the pronouncer's mouth, so to speak, annoys everyone and helps no one. Suppose, for example, that you ask a pronouncer to approve of a pronunciation that "forces out" the vowel behind a stubborn schwa. In doing so, you ask the pronouncer to approve of a mispronunciation of the word. In essence, you are asking the pronouncer to mispronounce that word – to violate his or her duty as a pronouncer – and you thereby insult the pronouncer.

Perhaps worse, you may create the appearance of poor sportsmanship on your part: Others may think that you are trying to get the pronouncer to approve of your incorrect pronunciation so that if you misspell, you can blame your mistake on that mispronunciation.

2. **Definition:** *The definition of your word is the most important single piece of information that you can request.*

a. First things first: If you know the word that you think that you heard, getting a definition helps you make sure that you heard the right word. If the definition that the pronouncer gives you matches the definition of the word that you believe the pronouncer to have said, then you have the right word in mind. In some ways, a definition is even better for this purpose than is a repronunciation: If you have problems hearing or recognizing a given sound and ask for a repronunciation, you may simply mishear the word twice in the same way. Asking for a definition gives you an independent way to confirm what word you heard.

b. Knowing the meaning of a word will give you clues as to what English elements or foreign roots make it up. Even if you have not studied foreign languages and are not directly familiar with a foreign word from which your word descends, you will likely have seen one or more of the word's elements in other English words. There is a good chance that you can take apart those words, put together the elements that match the meaning and sound of your word, and reconstruct your word. (For example, although I cannot read Greek from any era, at the 1994 nationals I was able to spell *hebephrenia* by taking elements from *hebetate* and *schizophrenia*.)

For these reasons, knowing a word's definition is so important that there is only a single, incredibly rare exception to the rule that you should always ask for it. (I will discuss that exception in the next section of this chapter.)

Some words have more than one definition. Not all bees will let you ask for alternate definitions, but if yours does, asking for alternate definitions may be a fresh way to get the information in *b)* above. Because a request for alternate definitions is a bit odd and because its answer can be time-consuming, save that request for when you need it. When a last-ditch effort is called for, however, it may be the question that saves you.

3. **Language of origin:** Finding out a word's language of origin helps you in two ways.

    a. Knowing the word's language of origin will help you "sound out" the word. Different languages that use the Roman alphabet spell different sounds in different ways, and different languages that use other alphabets or characters are transliterated into English in different ways. Knowing which language a word comes from will help you figure out how the word should look "on the page," letting you know which ways to spell the word's sounds are plausible and which are not.

       ▪ Of course, to use this information effectively, you need to be familiar with how different languages look on the page. The only way to gain this familiarity is to read and study enough that you encounter many words from many languages.

       ▪ Knowing how a word should look on the page is especially important if your bee includes a written test: During most written tests, contestants are not allowed to ask questions, so you cannot ask whether a specific root or English element (see below) gave rise to your word. Because during a written test you will not have access to this specific information, information about the more general patterns that a word follows is the best that you will be able to get.

         ▪ As far as written tests go, language-of-origin information is *even more* important if your test is multiple-choice: If your test is prepared correctly, only one available spelling for each word will be correct. The chances are overwhelming that the correct choice is the one that most closely follows the patterns of the word's language of origin. (See the discussion of "candidate spellings" on pages 37–38, in Chapter II's section on deduction, for more information about how your thought process in this situation should work.)

b. Especially if you have already been given the word's definition, knowing the word's language of origin may help you recall specific roots in that language.

4. **Confirmation of specific root word:** Hearing your word and its meaning may remind you of an English word element or foreign word that matches the sound in the word's pronunciation and the meaning in its definition. Asking whether that element or word gave rise to your word will give you important, specific information about how your word is spelled in English. (Think of specific roots as the concrete examples underlying the general patterns addressed by the language-of-origin question.)

This information won't always give you everything that you need to spell the word. For example, vowels connecting word elements may still be troublesome (think of *-iform* versus *-oform*). Also, there are multiple widely-accepted sets of rules for transliterating words from some languages, such as Yiddish and Russian, that use non-Roman alphabets. Even when only one set of rules is widely accepted, its subset of rules applicable to your word's roots may not exclude all incorrect options. (Most notably, Greek *αι* [*ai*] entered Latin almost always as *ae*, and Latin *ae* may come into English as either *ae* or *e*. The same goes for Greek *οι* [*oi*]: *οι/oi* became Latin *oe*, which can become in English either *oe* or *e*.)

11

5. **Use of your word in a sentence:** *An example of how your word is used in a sentence is the least helpful piece of information that you can request.*

With minor exceptions that I will discuss in a moment, using your word in a sentence serves only two purposes: First, it allows you to hear the word again, a benefit that a repronunciation would provide at less cost of time and effort. Second, the word's context in the sentence gives you some clue about what it means — but if a definition is what you are after, you might as well just ask for it and get more precise information. Thus, especially at nationals, where as of this writing competitors must spell within a fixed time, **you have little or no reason to request that the pronouncer use your word in a sentence.** Although I have no evidence indicating why spelling bees continue to allow spellers to ask for a word's use in a sentence, I suspect that there are only two reasons: Honoring such requests is 1) a longstanding spelling bee tradition at all levels of competition and 2) a way for spelling bees to prove to their detractors that words given in competition are useful in everyday life.

There are only two ways in which you can use this request to your possible advantage. One is always inadvisable, and one can be advisable if you think and study in ways that may make it useful.

a. At competitions in which your time for thinking is not fixed, you may be able to stall for time by requesting that the pronouncer use your word in a sentence. *Do not do this.* Everyone will know what you are doing, and you will exasperate the pronouncer, the judges, and the audience alike. Besides, the pronouncer's reading the sentence will likely distract you from the thinking that you had hoped to do, and you will not be able to put the time that you buy (or rather steal) to very productive use.

b. Spellers with highly developed visual learning skills may be able to remember words from seeing them in print in specific phrases. (This ability is an example of "chunking": The context of a piece of information can make recalling or reconstructing that information easier than it would be if the information occurred by itself or with random other information.)

    i. Some words usually or always occur as part of a fixed or "frozen" phrase. For example, *avail* almost always occurs in either "avail [one]sel[f] of" or "to no avail." Hearing this phrase may remind you of reading the phrase, helping you visualize the word as it appeared on the page when you read it.

    ii. Especially at higher levels of competition, there is some chance that words and their sentences come from a source previously used by the authority running your competition. These sources are sometimes available to spellers either from the sponsor itself or through informal channels such as study groups. Examples from the SNSB are its Consolidated Word List (see pages 64 and 109–110 below) and Sponsor Bee Guides (see pages 65 and 110 below) from previous years of competition. If your local competition does not rely on Scripps for its word lists, it may publish its old lists and/or reuse words and their sentences from those lists. If you have studied one or more of these sources, you may recognize your word's sentence from there.

To summarize: **If you possess very good visualization skills and use them in studying, and especially if you**

have studied lists previously used by the organization running your competition, asking for your word's use in a sentence may be helpful to you. Otherwise, it is a waste of your time and that of everyone around you.

These are the questions that you are allowed to ask and the information that they give you. The next step is to determine what order of questions enables you to make the best possible use of the information that you receive.

2: At the Microphone
WHEN TO ASK WHAT – AND WHEN TO MOVE ON AND SPELL

As you practice and compete, you will quickly find that some questions are more useful when asked before or after others. (For example, asking for a definition before asking about one or more specific roots lets you narrow down which specific roots to ask about, because roots with meanings that match the definition are usually the only viable options.)

That said, there is no need to ask the same questions in the same order every single time. If you know from a word's pronunciation and definition what word it is and how to spell it, then there is no need to ask about roots or request alternate pronunciations or definitions. Gather your thoughts by offering one final test pronunciation, and then spell the word.

Asking questions about a word is like crying "Wolf!": It's good to do so if you actually need more information or if there actually is a wolf, but if you lose favor with the judges or your fellow townsfolk by doing so when you don't need to, they may grow tired of you and refuse to help you in your hour of true need. Except for requests for a definition, save your questions – and with them, the good graces of the judges – for when you need them.

There are few things more irritating to judges, audience members, and fellow competitors than a speller who clearly knows a word but continues to ask unnecessary questions. A speller who asks about specific roots despite clearly knowing that a word does in fact descend from them will be perceived as a show-off (yes, I did this with *mesomorphic* in 1993). A speller who adheres to a predetermined, unvarying order of questions regardless of their necessity will come across as unhealthily compulsive and/or as desperate to placate an overbearing coach.

The following procedure lays out the order of permitted questions in which those questions make themselves most useful. It is not a single predetermined list of questions; there is no need to ask every question every time. Think of it as a verbal version of a flowchart showing different paths to take under different circumstances. (Speaking of flowcharts, I have put together one that summarizes and visually represents this order of questions; the flowchart appears at the end of this section.)

After you approach the microphone, indicate your readiness to the pronouncer by stopping and looking toward him or her. Watch the pronouncer's face as closely as you can without distracting from your listening as you hear your word for the first time.

Once you hear the word, begin your questioning by confirming what word you heard, either by asking for a repronunciation or by offering a test pronunciation.

As discussed above, confirming the word's pronunciation will confirm what word you've been given and will bring into focus the subject matter of your further questions.

Next, even if you think that you know the word, ask for the word's definition under all circumstances except one.

Even if you know how to spell the word that you believe the pronouncer to have said, it's good to get independent confirmation of what word the pronouncer actually *did* say. Pronouncers and judges understand this fact and are always happy to give a definition. (Before someone else brings it up, I'll admit it: Although I confirmed my hearing of my winning word, *antediluvian*, with a test pronunciation, I did not ask for a definition. The footage doesn't lie, and it speaks of dangerous behavior on my part.)

Spell without asking for a definition ONLY IF
a) the rules of your bee require the pronouncer to distinguish between homonyms,
b) you know that your word has a homonym,
c) the pronouncer did not distinguish between the homonyms,
d) you <u>do</u> know how to spell at least one homonym,
AND
e) EITHER
  i) there is at least one homonym that you do not know how to spell
  OR
  ii) you do not know which spelling corresponds to which homonym.

For example, suppose that *a*) you're given the word ['käm·plə·mənt] in a bee that follows the standard rules, *b*) you know how to spell at least one of the homonyms *compliment* and *complement*, and *c*) you know that one means "an expression of approval" and/or that the other means "that which completes" but *d*) you can't remember which is which or can't remember how to spell one of them.

16

Asking for a definition will distinguish between the homonyms and force you to spell a specific word, leaving you with at best a 50-percent chance of spelling it correctly. In contrast, the standard rules require judges to accept the correct spelling of either homonym if they do not distinguish between the two. Therefore, correctly spelling one of the homonyms without asking questions will force the judges to accept your spelling (whether immediately or if they eliminate you and you appeal). Be advised that this tactic amounts to "gaming the system" and will frustrate the judges. Use it only if you absolutely have to.

At this point, if you know what word you have been given and how to spell it, do not take up any more time. Reconfirm what word you have been given by offering a test pronunciation, and then spell the word.

On the other hand, if you are not sure how to spell the word that you have been given, the first step in figuring it out is to analyze it, that is, to break it up into its elements so that you can decipher it piece by piece.

A word's elements include its main body (which may itself have subparts) and any prefixes or suffixes that the word may have. In your study or other reading, you may have encountered some or all of these elements as they occur in other words. With practice, you may become able to recognize previously encountered elements as soon as you hear a word defined or even pronounced.

If you think that you recognize an element or root of your word, and especially if you remember that element's or root's meaning, it may be tempting to begin by asking whether your word is derived from that element or root. For the moment, however, I recommend merely keeping that information in mind as an educated guess. Before trying to confirm that guess,

ask for your word's language of origin. Getting your word's language of origin first is helpful for a number of reasons:

1. Even if your guess about your word's root is right, the root may have passed through another language and in the process changed before coming into English. For example, if you ask whether part of a word comes from a given Latin root, the answer will be "yes" whether the element came directly from Latin or went through, say, French between Latin and English. Knowing what path the element took into English will help you figure out whether its spelling *a*) likely "tracks" that of the root that you have in mind or instead *b*) has likely been modified according to the patterns prevalent in whatever language it went through between the root's language and English.

2. If you have multiple possible roots in mind, knowing a word element's path into English may help you shorten your mental list of options by eliminating roots that haven't passed through (at least one of) the language(s) listed.

3. Hearing the word's language of origin may even jog your memory by reminding you of specific roots from that language.

4. When you ask for your word's language of origin, you will get information about all parts of that word. Getting this information sooner rather than later will give your mind more time to work on the word's other parts, even if you're devoting your conscious attention to one element at a time.

If you are familiar with one or more English elements or foreign roots that match a meaning within the word's definition, sounds within its pronunciation, and the language-of-origin information that you have been given, then **for each of those elements and/or roots** (or, more precisely, for as many of them as it takes to get accurate and complete information for each part of your word), **ask whether it gave rise to your word.**

1. If you have different roots in mind for different parts of the word (*e.g.*, *automobile*, ultimately from Greek *autos*, "self," + Latin *mobilis*, "movable"), it is best to ask about them one at a time. If you ask about more than one in a single question, then you risk getting an unhelpful "yes and no" answer if one of your guesses is correct and one is incorrect. (Even worse, a judge who is a stickler for formal logic might give you a blanket "yes" if your question uses "or" or a blanket "no" if your question uses "and"!)

2. Be sure to specify the meaning and, if you know it, the language of the root that you are asking about. Do so for two reasons: First, providing this information will let the judges know which root you have in mind and will thereby help them answer your question. Second, by volunteering this information you will provide evidence that you have a good-faith basis for your question, as opposed to merely grasping at straws by making a thinly veiled effort to sound out the word.

If your questions about specific roots give you information about the immediate "ancestor" of every part of the word, then you are in good shape. Gather your thoughts, reconfirm the word's identity by offering a test pronunciation, and spell the word.

If parts of the word are still unfamiliar or if a word element changed after taking the form of the root you had in mind, examine the word more closely in light of its language(s) of origin.

Focus on the syllables that you did not immediately recognize as belonging to a specific English element and/or foreign root. Think about these syllables again, keeping in mind the language(s) of origin that you have been given. See whether any syllables or groups of syllables remind you of a root in any language of your word's origin or of any elements in other English words, especially English words that descend from that language. As before, ask about any roots that come to mind.

If the word's definition and language of origin do not remind you of any roots or if the word does not come from any roots or elements that you had in mind, then you are probably faced with the unenviable task of having to sound out the word as well as you can.

Your main tasks from this point forward are to get as much information about the word's sound as possible and to figure out how that sound is spelled according to the patterns most common in the word's language of origin. Of course, if the answers to your questions remind you of more guesses about a word's specific roots, then you should not hesitate to ask about them.

To begin sounding out the word and making an educated guess about how it is spelled, ask for any alternate pronunciations of the word.

As noted above, this question is especially useful for clarifying stubborn schwas, both between word elements and within word elements themselves — but don't try to force them out.

Once you have information about the word's language of origin, the alternate-pronunciation question becomes even more useful. Most languages have multiple ways to spell certain sounds, but not all of those spellings are consistent with *all* of the *English* pronunciations that you are given. As a rule, the only spellings that stand a chance of being correct are those that fit the patterns set by your word's language of origin *and* are consistent with all of your word's English pronunciations.

If an alternate pronunciation reminds you of one or more possible roots in the word's language of origin, ask about them. If you have found a match for each element of your word, move on and spell.

If the alternate pronunciations still leave some sounds unclear and do not help you think of any roots whose spelling clears them up, consider asking whether your word has any alternate definitions.

If your competition's rules do not permit this question, do not irritate the judges by asking it. Also, use your time wisely: If your time at the microphone is limited, as it is at nationals as of this writing, then you probably should not use that time to get more information that you will then have even less time to process and use. Instead, use your remaining time to draw what conclusions you can from the information that you have.

In theory, the alternate-definitions question belongs with the regular request for a definition: Its purpose, like one purpose of the definition request, is to remind you of English word elements or foreign roots.

I save it for this point, however, because you should ask it only when you're really in trouble: It's an unusual question that makes you look strange when you ask it, and if your word does have alternate definitions, they will take some time to provide, so asking this question when it isn't necessary will likely alienate the judges – and, if your competition features time limits, will cost you time that you might need for finishing your spelling. If you are at a total loss, however, an alternate definition may give you one last shot at finding a specific root.

21

If you have asked for alternate definitions and if those definitions remind you of one or more specific elements or roots, ask about them. If the answers you get confirm the ancestry of each part of your word, move on and spell.

If all else fails, if your time at the microphone is not limited, and only if your learning style makes it helpful to do so (see above), ask the pronouncer to use your word in a sentence.

At this point, you have gotten all the information that you can and done with it everything that you can. It is time to gather your thoughts – especially those about how your word's language of origin appears in print – and spell the word.

Spelling the Word

When you are ready (or as ready as you'll ever be) to spell, **give one final test pronunciation as you visualize the word or your best guess at it.**

As long as you spell carefully, **how you pace yourself while you spell is up to you: Pace yourself using whatever method best helps you keep track of your place in the word.** Some contestants maintain their progress through a word by reciting letters at a constant tempo. Others group letters syllable by syllable. Still others group them by etymological element. If your instincts do not automatically select a pacing method, feel free to test your instincts' compatibility with each of a variety of methods as you practice.

"Putting It All Together"

The following flowchart provides a comprehensive "road map" of your encounter with any word that you face in competition, regardless of both the word's level of objective difficulty and your level of subjective familiarity with it.

If you've ever studied computer programming, you've likely seen flowcharts in which parallelogram-shaped boxes contain requests for some sort of data "input." This flowchart's parallelograms are much the same, showing questions to ask the pronouncer in order to obtain or confirm important information. In turn, diamond-shaped boxes show questions to ask yourself in order to determine what to do next, and oblong boxes show other actions to perform.

If you haven't seen many flowcharts before or if this one just seems a bit convoluted at first sight, here are two tips for quickly getting a good grasp of it:

- **Before you first use the flowchart in practice, read through it a few times**, each time following a different branch of the "decision tree" formed by your answers to the chart's "yes/no" questions.

- **When you begin to use the flowchart in practice, keep it open in front of you** so that you can *a)* practice asking the specific questions that it recommends – whether those questions are directed to the pronouncer or to yourself – and *b)* see how well your existing thought processes "map onto" the structure that the flowchart provides.

Because this flowchart is essentially a formalization and streamlining of the "word detective" work that your mind is already trying to do, you will likely need only a little practice to become proficient in its use — and with that proficiency will come both an increased comfort with this method and an increased willingness to trust yourself when applying it.

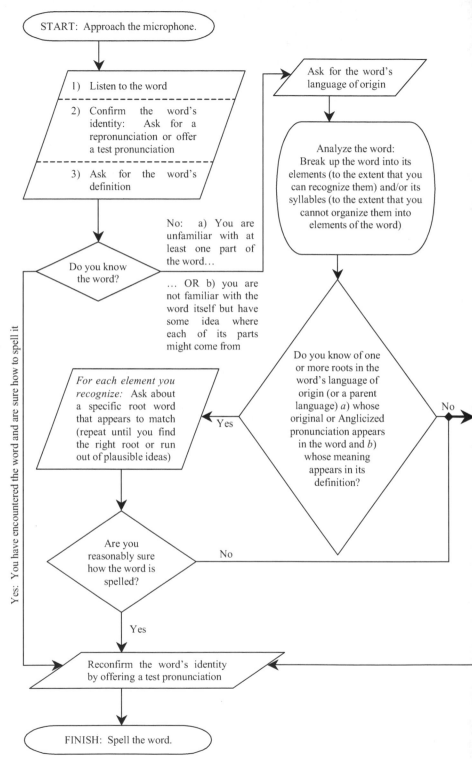

START: Approach the microphone.

1) Listen to the word
- -
2) Confirm the word's identity: Ask for a repronunciation or offer a test pronunciation
- -
3) Ask for the word's definition

Do you know the word?

No: a) You are unfamiliar with at least one part of the word…

… OR b) you are not familiar with the word itself but have some idea where each of its parts might come from

Ask for the word's language of origin

Analyze the word: Break up the word into its elements (to the extent that you can recognize them) and/or its syllables (to the extent that you cannot organize them into elements of the word)

Do you know of one or more roots in the word's language of origin (or a parent language) *a*) whose original or Anglicized pronunciation appears in the word and *b*) whose meaning appears in its definition?

No

Yes

For each element you recognize: Ask about a specific root word that appears to match (repeat until you find the right root or run out of plausible ideas)

Are you reasonably sure how the word is spelled?

No

Yes: You have encountered the word and are sure how to spell it

Yes

Reconfirm the word's identity by offering a test pronunciation

FINISH: Spell the word.

24

"For emergency use only":
Ask these questions only if you're genuinely stuck.
Otherwise, save your time and the judges' patience
for when you really need them.

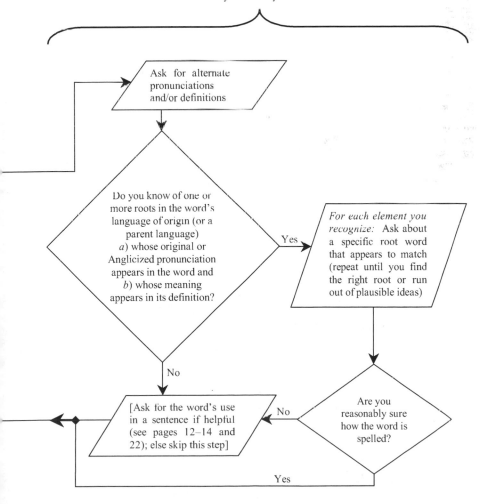

No matter how hard you try to stay calm on stage or how emotionally detached you try to be, you will in all likelihood experience stress during competition.

Different people experience stress in different ways, and different methods of stress management work for different people. For this reason, I have only a single and admittedly vague suggestion for managing the physical and emotional effects of stress during competition: **Before competition season begins, do your best to find one or more stress management techniques that work for you. Make sure that all of them can be used on stage without disrupting or distracting from the competition. Then practice them and use them.**[3]

When it comes to intellectual outlooks that affect how much stress you experience in the first place, however, I have two specific suggestions. Each of them is a way to **reevaluate your emotions in light of the facts that really matter.**

1. **As you advance to later rounds of a bee and higher levels of competition, your fear of misspelling should *decrease*, not increase.**

   Many contestants get more and more nervous as a given competition progresses and as they advance to higher and higher levels of competition. These contestants have it backward. Although it's true that the difficulty of the

---

[3] For example, in 1992 or 1993, I improvised a crude breath control technique that I recognize in hindsight to be a form of "tense and relax": Inhale deeply but quietly, and then quietly exhale while restricting the flow of air by tightening your throat. I found this method to be quite useful in 1994, but before you assume that it will work for you, try it as you practice — and try to find or develop something better.

words given, the likelihood of your misspelling, and the number of people watching all increase as competition goes on, these increases don't constitute reasons to become nervous – especially given that the likelihood of misspelling increases for *every* competitor in inverse proportion to his or her aptitude and preparation. Unless something is seriously wrong, no one will punish you if you misspell.[4] At most, you will feel temporarily embarrassed that you missed and regretful about the spelling that you chose. Yet even these emotions should decrease rather than increase as competition progresses: **As you advance farther, you have proven yourself more, you have less left to prove, and whatever word you miss will likely be more difficult — so you should feel less nervous about the prospect of misspelling, and you should feel less embarrassed or regretful if you do misspell.**[5]

Of course, if this is the way in which you think about competitions, and especially if you made nationals the previous year and/or have otherwise built up a reputation to defend, your classroom- and school-level bees will be nerve-racking.[6] At lower levels, however, the words will be

---

[4] *Students:* If your parents or peers are threatening you or have in the past harmed you for misspelling, **tell someone** such as a guidance counselor or, if the threats or harm are severe enough, a law enforcement officer. Although this never happened to me, I know of a small number of people to whom it has happened. These people sought and found help, and in each case the offender was punished.

[5] Disclosure: I have made this argument in several interviews that have been previously published, with the most notable version of my remarks appearing on page 112 of James Maguire's book *American Bee: The National Spelling Bee and the Culture of Word Nerds* (Emmaeus, Pa.: Rodale/Holtzbrinck, 2006, ISBN-13 #978-1-5948-6214-4).

[6] I first encountered this consequence by experiencing it during the 1994 competition season. My thoughts on this matter, too, have been

simpler and should be easier to handle despite your nervousness. Think of it this way: You're going to get nervous either way, so you might as well get nervous when you're facing easy words. When the thought processes that you're using aren't as finely tuned, nerves are less likely to "tip the balance" from a correct spelling to an incorrect one.

2. **Don't let other competitors, their skill, their past performance, or their reputation intimidate you — neither they nor anything about them can make you misspell.**

A spelling bee is unlike most other competitions in that whether you succeed (spell correctly) has nothing to do with whether your "opponents" succeed or fail. For example, it differs from a baseball game, in which the pitcher tries to throw the ball past the batter and the batter tries to hit the ball past the fielders. If you've ever played on a baseball team, you may remember the infield chatter "No batter, no batter," with which fielders encourage a struggling pitcher to disregard a batter's hitting skills and focus on putting the ball in the strike zone. In a spelling bee, there *is* "no batter"; there *is* no one else whose skills can affect your performance. Your sole task is to give an accurate spelling – the equivalent of throwing an accurate pitch – and if you do so, then you will stay in the competition regardless of how well or poorly the contestants around you spell.

Instead, you and your fellow spellers are in an endurance contest: Each of you is trying to last as long as possible against your common foe, the word list, and whoever lasts

---

previously published, most notably at page 112 of *American Bee* (see note 5 above).

longest wins. Think of each round as a game of blackjack in which each player is trying to match or beat the dealer's hand but in which no player is trying to outdo any other.[7]

Short of interference with another person's spelling, which constitutes unsportsmanlike conduct and is therefore punishable by disqualification under the SNSB's suggested rules[8], **no speller can affect how long another speller lasts in absolute terms**[9] **— all you can do is make yourself last as long as possible. Whether that happens to be longer than other contestants last is secondary.** For specific tips about facing professionally coached competitors, see the end of Chapter III's section 3.

It can be helpful (and, for many people with "spelling instincts," it's irresistible) to listen to other spellers' words and get in some last-minute mental practice by considering what questions you would ask and how you would spell those words. Whether other spellers get their words right is irrelevant to this task, however, because in the end either they or the pronouncer will let everyone know their words' correct spelling. All you should do – and all you really can do – is to **do your best and let other people worry about how well they do.**

---

[7] Again, my use of this analogy has been previously published, most notably at page 113 of *American Bee* (see note 5 above).

[8] See, for example, "Disqualifications for reasons other than clear misspelling" in Rule 6 of "Rules for Local Spelling Bees" at URL in note 2 above.

[9] It is true that if your competition uses a single, continuous word list (*i.e.*, one without predetermined round breaks), a previous contestant's correct or incorrect spelling will affect which word you receive in the next round. However, that effect can help you as easily as it can hurt you, and in any case, the other speller does not know what his or her next word would be, so he or she is unable to knowingly affect what word you receive.

Now that you know what you'll be doing when you're on stage, let's take a look at the processes that your mind uses when performing these tasks – and, with them, the areas of aptitude whose development will help you refine those processes as fully as possible.

CHAPTER II:
THE SKILLS OF SUCCESSFUL SPELLERS

During my involvement in and with competitive spelling, I have observed numerous similarities between competitive spelling and the use of the classical scientific method.

Generally speaking, "book study" for spelling competition is a process of collecting information of two types: *a*) the spellings of specific words and *b*) patterns governing the spellings of multiple words that you've learned. Competition-style spelling itself, whether in drills or in an actual bee, is a process of following those spellings or applying those patterns in order to predict the spelling of an unknown (or at least unexpected) word – in other words, to generate a hypothesis about how the word should be spelled.

The rest of the analogy to the scientific method is obvious to people who have ever watched a spelling bee or been on stage themselves: You test your hypothesis by spelling the word, and its rejection or confirmation comes when you hear or don't hear the bell!

Broadly speaking, there are four skills on which you will rely as you study and spell: **memorization, recollection, induction,** and **deduction**.

1. The process of **memorization** discussed in this chapter corresponds to the simplest of that term's various senses: the making of an initial mental record of what you encounter. To ask "How good are you at memorizing things?" is to ask "On average, what fraction of what you encounter do you remember?" It's important to note that this question means not only "How many things do you remember?" but "How much do you remember about each thing that you remember?"

31

In preparing for competition, you will likely commit to memory both specific and general information: the spelling of specific words, the spelling of English elements and foreign roots that occur in multiple related words, and patterns governing the spelling of multiple words that are unrelated but come from the same language.

As for where to find general information to memorize, you may encounter it in a pre-prepared form, such as in etymological dictionaries or lists of spelling rules and generalizations, or you may develop it on your own. The process of distilling general rules from the examination of large sets of specific data is known as induction, and I discuss it more below.

2. **Recollection** is the quick and reliable accessing of mental records that you made through memorization. Your ability to recall an already-formed memory depends on several factors.

First is the number of properties of a memory that your mind associates with other observations or memories – in other words, the number of ways in which you can be reminded of it. Second is the number of memories that your mind recognizes as having each property in common with that memory – in other words, the number of memories that can remind you of it in each way.

Putting these first two factors together shows that you can recall a memory directly or indirectly: You can recognize that a situation that you're in shares a property with that memory, or you can recognize that your situation shares a property with a memory that shares a *different* property with the memory that you eventually recall.

The point is that the more detailed each of your memories is, the more ways there are for you to be reminded of it. Therefore, it's more likely that something that you notice or are thinking about will remind you of it, and it's more likely that some other memory that's been "triggered" will do the same thing. The result is that the more detailed each of your memories is, the fewer "steps" it will take, on average, for you to recall a given memory.

The third factor affecting your recollection ability is the speed with which each of these steps happens – in other words, how quickly a situation or memory directly reminds you of another memory.

If you want to decrease the amount of time it takes to recall a memory, then, there are two available ways: You can speed up each step that recalling the memory requires, but you can also reduce the number of steps required, either by forming a wider variety of memories or by making each of your memories contain more information that it can then have in common with other observations and memories.

Therefore, there are three basic ways to improve your abilities of recollection: You can **increase the variety of memories that you have**, **increase the detail of the memories that you form**, and/or **increase the speed at which you associate observations with memories and memories with other memories**. (Notice that the first two of these ways also involve improving your memorization skills.)

Just as you will commit both specific and general information to memory when you study, you will (if all goes well) recall both types of information when you are at the microphone. Obviously, if you know a word, its pronunciation will remind you of its spelling, and the word's definition will confirm that reminder. Even if you don't know a word, however, recollection will help you in two ways. First, the pronunciation of a syllable or group of syllables may remind you of a word element. Second, the word's language of origin will remind you of that language's patterns governing words containing the sounds that you're given.

3. Roughly speaking, **induction** consists of the examination of the data that you have and the formulation of a general rule that fits those data as well as it can while still being concise enough that you can "hold it in your head" for practical use. In your preparation, you will use inductive reasoning on a variety of levels.

   Sometimes you will use induction to find the spelling and meaning of specific English elements. For a simple example, if you study words such as *anthropology*, *anthropomorphic*, and *philanthropy* and their definitions, you may realize that the English element *anthrop-* or *anthropo-* means "human being." This way, you can figure out the same general rule that someone with training in Greek might have memorized from a vocabulary book: When a word's pronunciation contains the syllables that the above words have in common, the word's definition relates to human beings, and the word comes from Greek, *-anthrop-* is the way to spell those syllables. (Of course, it's always good to check your observations against the dictionary, which will tell you directly that this element is derived from the Greek word ανθρωπος [*anthrōpos*].) This is the "major premise" that you will use when you rely on deductive reasoning to figure out the spelling of an unfamiliar word.

   At other times, you will use induction to find patterns that span across multiple words coming from a given language, governing the spelling or transliteration patterns that the source language as a whole follows. Sometimes, only people formally trained in linguistics (if even they) can articulate the principles underlying a language's spelling patterns. As a result, your inductive reasoning at this level will often be "fuzzier" and less formal than is your reasoning about particular word elements. (For this reason, it's sometimes distinguished from step-by-step induction by referring to it as "pattern recognition.") However, if you've encountered many words derived from that source language – especially "loan words" adopted without alteration – you may be able to infer (and later apply) a set of patterns even if you can't formally state them.

Some of the rules that you identify will be prescriptive, telling you what must be the case: "All Hawaiian syllables end in vowels." Others will be proscriptive, telling you what cannot be the case: "Hawaiian words cannot have consecutive consonants." Often, a prescriptive rule can be paraphrased in proscriptive form or vice versa: "Hawaiian syllables cannot end in consonants"; "Hawaiian words with multiple consonants must have at least one vowel between those consonants." In turn, rules can often be combined, yielding rules that are more comprehensive while being no more difficult to remember: "Hawaiian words must have at least one vowel after every consonant."

Some rules of each type are not absolutely uniform but rather take the form of recommendations of varying strength. For two classic examples, "words directly from Latin are almost always spelled with *c* rather than with *k*," and "words directly from classical Greek are almost always spelled with *ph* rather than with *f*." There are less "hard and fast" examples that are too numerous to mention, but the general principle is that they tell you how a certain sound is (or is not) spelled a majority or plurality of the time, given conditions such as a word's language of origin and the sound's position within that word. It is good to figure out as many of these recommendations as possible, because they are what you will have to apply in most situations when you have to make an educated guess about how to "sound out" a word.

4. **Deduction** is the application of a general rule to a situation in which specific facts are observed or given, with the goal of finding out some other specific fact about the situation. Formally speaking, deduction is an argument of the form "If A [is true], then B [is true]; A [is true]; therefore, B [is true]." It is through inductive reasoning (and/or memorization from outside sources) that you learn rules of the form "If A, then B." Deductive reasoning applies these rules to specific cases in which the conditions listed in statement A are satisfied.

The simplest form of deduction involves how to spell a word that descends from a root that you've figured out or memorized. Returning to the example of *-anthrop-* discussed above: Suppose that you are given the word *anthropogenesis*, which comes from Greek and means "the origin and development of humankind," but have never encountered it before. If you're familiar with the rule governing how to spell words that are pronounced with those syllables, that have to do with human beings, and that are of Greek origin, you can easily figure out how to spell the first half of the word. The word's pronunciation, definition, and language of origin satisfy all of the conditions for the rule's applicability, so if the rule holds true, then the conclusion about the word's spelling will follow.

Deduction can help you apply rules about more general linguistic patterns as well. If you can remember patterns governing how a sound is usually spelled (or not spelled) given a word's language of origin and the sound's position in that word, those patterns will help point you in the right direction (or away from the wrong direction) when you're at the microphone.

An alternative form of deductive reasoning is useful for testing a spelling that you're considering (what I'll call a "candidate spelling" by analogy to the chess term "candidate move," which I learned from U.S. Chess Federation Original Life Master Leonard Dickerson). This alternative method is to begin with that spelling and "think backward." If you've studied geometry, you may be familiar with the concept of "indirect proof," in which you prove that a statement is not true by showing that if it were true, its implications would contradict one or more statements given as true. You can do the same with a candidate spelling, asking yourself whether it contradicts rules or recommendations of which you're aware – and rejecting it or considering it less likely if it does.[10]

Working backward from candidate spellings is also helpful when you're trying to decide between multiple candidate spellings for a word. Choosing the best candidate spelling is a more involved version of deciding whether a single candidate spelling is plausible: Keeping each spelling in mind, go through each of the source language's "hard and fast" rules that come to mind and reject any of the spellings that violate any of the rules. For the spellings that remain, go through the positive and negative "recommendations" for spelling in a given language and see which spelling obeys the most positive recommendations and disobeys the fewest negative recommendations.

---

[10] If you've watched the national finals on television, you may have seen spellers "finger-writing" or "typing" candidate spellings in the air or on their placards. Many of these spellers are likely attempting to improve their visualization of one or more candidate spellings so that they can see how well those spellings fit the patterns that they have observed.

"Thinking backward" is especially useful if you're having trouble thinking of explicit rules or generalizations that would help you in a particular situation. When you have to sound out a word and have a candidate spelling in mind, asking yourself "Does this look right?" consists primarily of asking yourself how well the spelling obeys the source language's patterns that you have subsconsciously or unconsciously recognized.

- **"What about intuition?": Instinctive deduction from previously recognized patterns?**

At times, you may simply have a "hunch" or "gut feeling" about how to spell a word based on the information you have. Although all of my formal training in psychology and cognitive science has been incidental to my study in other fields, my experience with spelling suggests that these "hunches" represent instinctive recollection and application of patterns that you've previously (and often instinctively) recognized and committed to memory.

In other words, I believe, the formation of a spelling "hunch" or intuition often consists of unconscious inductive reasoning from your existing knowledge followed by unconscious deductive reasoning applying the resulting patterns to the pronunciation that you are given. At other times, it may consist of unconscious deduction from rules or patterns that you've studied as formally articulated principles but that aren't at the forefront of your mind as you're at the microphone.

I could be wrong about the source of at least some of these intuitions: During the press conference following his national championship in 2000, George Thampy famously described hearing a voice, which he perceived as the voice of God, telling him how to spell the first two syllables of the word *emmetropia*. If you have a Supreme Being on your side, more power to you — but as competition season draws near, begins, and progresses, remember the maxim that God helps those who help themselves.

Of course, to apply a rule or pattern that you've previously noticed, you must recall it either consciously or unconsciously. To recall it, you must have consciously or unconsciously committed it to memory after recognizing it, just as you would if you had learned an English element or foreign root from an etymological dictionary. Therefore, **figuring out a word that you don't immediately recognize involves skills on both levels: The "higher-order" functions of induction to start with and deduction to finish with are useless without the "lower-order" functions of memorization and recollection.**

The following table shows the order in which your preparation and competition draw on these skills. The arrows leading from induction to memorization and from recollection to deduction are dashed because they are not always applicable: You draw on induction and perform deduction only when you have not memorized a word and therefore cannot recall it but instead can only make an educated guess about its spelling.

	Input (from data): Study of existing words	Output (to hypothesis): Deciding how to spell a word in practice or competition
Maintenance of existing information	**Memorization** of particular word, element, or spelling rule/pattern	**Recollection** of existing memory about particular word, element, or spelling rule/pattern
Generation of new information	**Induction:** Recognition of word element or spelling rule/pattern	**Deduction:** Application of previously recognized rule/pattern to generate spelling

Each of the two skills that you will use when studying (memorization and induction) has a "mirror image" that you will use when practicing and competing (recollection and deduction, respectively). The metaphor of a mirror image is more than a cliché: Although the two images relate to the same subject matter, each is in many ways the opposite of the other. The differences between them lead to differences in the ways in which their incorrect application – or even their correct application to the wrong information – can lead you into error.

1. Memorization vs. recollection

Although it's true that exceptional ability in the area of memory formation is often found together with exceptional ability in the field of recollection, at least part of this perceived correlation is attributable to "sampling bias" in that neither ability is likely to display itself and be noticed unless the other is also present. In any event, these skills are technically two independent things.

a. Memorization

It's possible for a person to have many memories but use only a few aspects of those memories to link them to what the person observes and other memories that the person has. If this is the case, the person may be reminded of those memories in only a few isolated situations, and in other contexts they may be entirely overlooked or "on the tip of the person's tongue."

b. Recollection

Likewise, it's possible for a person not to have an especially large number of memories but to be able to associate many aspects of those memories with other memories and current observations. Such a person will "get a lot of mileage" out of what memories he or she does have: When faced with a given situation, he or she may be able to apply at least as many memories as could someone with more numerous memories but more limited ability to use any given memory. However, this result will occur only if an appropriate memory gets "triggered" in the first place, and when fewer memories are available, that initial step will be less likely to occur.

2. Induction vs. deduction

a. Induction

Inductive reasoning can sometimes lead you astray even if you properly apply it to the information that you have. Specifically, you can go wrong with induction if you are missing one or more pieces of information that are inconsistent with the rule or pattern that you have inferred. Any rule or generalization formulated without accounting for this inconsistent information will be imprecise. Such a rule may recommend an incorrect spelling of an unfamiliar word even if your deductive application of the rule to that word is itself entirely correct.

- Some pieces of information inconsistent with your rule appear to be counterexamples only because the rule that you've come up with isn't refined enough. In truth, these data are good examples of a more refined rule. Once you encounter enough of them, they will lead you to observe that better rule.

   For example, suppose that your study of Japanese words teaches you that all Japanese syllables end in a vowel or a nasal consonant. You might draw the generalization that all English transliterations of

Japanese words follow the same rule — unless you also know that when a consonant at the start of a Japanese syllable is "geminated" (articulated for longer than usual), many English transliterations indicate that fact by doubling the consonant. Examples include *Hokkaido*, *hokkigai*, *hokku*, *Nippon*, *teppan*, and *natto*. (In these transliterations, not all of which have entries in *Webster's Third*, the first of the doubled consonants serves as the end of the previous syllable in the English pronunciation.)

- Other words represent genuine "freak" exceptions.

Suppose that after studying words such as *acromegaly*, *Acropolis*, *acrobat*, and *acrophobia* you draw the generalization that the κ (kappa) in Greek [-]ακρο- ("extreme," "high") is always transliterated as the Romance *c*. When attempting to apply this rule deductively, you'll be in for an unpleasant surprise if you're asked to spell *akropodion* or *akrochordite* — two very rare exceptions to an almost completely uniform rule. (In fact, they are the only words that I can find in *Webster's Third* that come from this root but do not have variant spellings using [-]*acr*-.) Neither word gives you any clue that it is any different from other words (let alone its fellow anatomical or geological terms, respectively) that use the same Greek root.

If you've encountered exceptions to what appear to be almost-universal rules, if you've checked the dictionary and determined those exceptions to be truly rare, and if you can't think of any refinement to the rule that would adequately explain them, then you're better off disregarding them and going with the majority rule when you're asked to spell an unfamiliar word. **When all else fails, sometimes you have to play the odds and hope that their prediction holds true in your specific case. The good news is that the more thoroughly you prepare, the better information you give yourself about what those odds really are.**

b. **Deduction**

Although deduction is popularly thought of as more reliable than induction, deductive reasoning works only to the extent that the premises from which one is working are true. Even if a rule ("major premise") always holds true and your theoretical understanding of it is perfect, you can go wrong with deduction if you misinterpret or overlook facts ("minor premises") to which you're attempting to apply the rule.

For example, if a word was originally Hawaiian or Japanese but passed through some other language before coming into English, it might not obey the quite rigid and phonetic rules of Hawaiian orthography or Japanese transliteration. If you forget the "intermediate language" information that the pronouncer gives you and instead treat the word as if it were "purely" Hawaiian or Japanese, you might well get it wrong.

What all of these skills have in common is that each can be improved with practice.

1. **Memory formation:** It's obvious that as you study more and pay closer attention to what you encounter in everyday life, you'll accumulate a greater store of factual information — but what's less obvious is that with practice you'll remember more in *relative* terms as well. As you study, not

only will you become more efficient at initially gathering information, but you'll remember a greater percentage of the information that you gather than you did before. This principle holds true whether you're encountering individual words or noticing patterns that govern multiple words.

2. **Recollection:** As you learn more words, you will find words that have elements and roots in common with the words that you already know. (Doing so amounts to increasing the variety of memories that you've formed.) As you think more about each word, whether during study or during simulated competition, you will become aware of more of its properties. (Doing so is a way of increasing the detail of each memory, enabling you to notice more words that share each word's properties.) When you practice spelling – figuring out which rules and generalizations apply to which words – the process of remembering those rules and generalizations will reinforce the pathways that you've built, so you'll become faster at using them. For all of these reasons, calling up memories will become an easier and faster process.

3. **Induction (rule or pattern recognition):** As you spend more time observing words and looking for common elements and similarities in their appearance on the page, you'll learn what to look for – what features of a word make it similar to other words – and you'll get faster at doing so. If you prepare seriously over an extended time, there's a good chance that this process will become instinctive. A good way to accelerate the process is to make your own study lists, grouping words with similar elements together so that their similarities and differences will become more clear. (See Chapter III's Part II, section 2, "The 'Spelling Notebook'," for details.)

4. **Deduction (rule or pattern application):** As you practice spelling, you will get better at applying the rules and patterns that you've learned. In addition to getting better at recalling them, you will find it easier to figure out which of them govern your word and what they say about it. As a result, you'll be able both to think more quickly (because you won't have to "fish around" as much) and to apply patterns more accurately, even to the point of being able to accept or reject candidate spellings instinctively.

5. **Intuition:** As your instincts for induction and deduction improve, you will begin to develop good spelling intuitions. As you practice, though, you should be careful to check your "hunches" against whatever rules you can consciously remember. Adding this technique to your practice routine enables you to refine your intuitions twice: first by checking them against the rules of which you're aware and then by seeing whether they've helped you spell a given practice word correctly.

Of course, no matter how good you are at these thought processes, they won't help you do well in competitive spelling unless you have substantial "raw material" of individual words, word elements, rules, and patterns for them to operate on. The next chapter will discuss where to find that raw material and what methods of organizing it enable you to develop these skills most effectively and efficiently.

CHAPTER III:
PREPARATION

Even casual participants in a hastily organized bar-room competition can apply the techniques in Chapter I and the skills in Chapter II to make the most of the knowledge that they already possess. The rest of this guide, however, is intended for people who are serious about making a long-term commitment to competitive spelling.

PART I: IS A LONG-TERM COMMITMENT FOR YOU?

Although the following "threshold questions" may seem obvious, it's good to pay serious attention to each of them individually – and both of them together – before devoting significant time, money, and/or other resources to competitive spelling:

1. **Do I have access to organized competition, and will it likely be around for the multiple years that it will take to become a seasoned spelling bee competitor?**

2. **Do I have enough spare time – or can I make enough time – to engage in serious preparation for organized competition?**

The vast majority of people who answer "yes" to both of these questions will be middle and junior high school students participating in the SNSB system. As of this writing, however, there exists some competitive spelling at the high school level, such as in the spelling and vocabulary division of Texas' University Interscholastic League (UIL) competition. In any case, if you can answer "yes" to both questions, the next step is to **ask whether you will find competitive spelling rewarding – that is, whether the goals that you have in** mind are goals that preparing for competitive spelling will help you realize.

1. **Bad reasons to get involved in competitive spelling**

   a. **Monetary or other prizes**

      It's easy for intelligent students eligible for SNSB competition to be tempted by the cash awards, scholarships, computers, expensive books, and other prizes awarded to top SNSB finishers. Indeed, in recent years these awards have grown beyond the wildest dreams (well, maybe not the wildest) of competitors in previous years.

      Yet only the very top finishers at nationals get prizes anywhere near sufficient to make their many hours of effort pay off as a business proposal. In terms of prize money per hour of study, at most only a handful of people in the nation will earn higher than minimum wage. Almost all of the rewards of study are intangible, and even the tangible ones are far from direct. For example, serious spelling competition gives you an edge in intellectual development, which increases your chances of getting into a better college and helps you do better once you're there, helping you get a higher-paying job — but each of these results depends on countless other factors as well. As these factors accumulate over the years, the effect of competitive spelling is diluted.

      In short: **If money is what you're looking for, put your time and skills to work elsewhere.** This advice applies even if you're too young to work according to the laws of your state, you get little to no allowance, and birthdays and holidays are your only other opportunities to get money. If you enjoy competitive spelling for other reasons, any money that you come by is of course nice to have, but to the extent that you consider it your primary reward, the chances are overwhelming that you are setting yourself up for frustration.

b. Short-run improvement in academic performance

As I discuss below, it is true that preparing for and competing in spelling bees will help you do better in school. It's also true that the skills you develop are fundamental to learning in general and will help you with a broad array of subjects. Finally, it's true that the improvement in your skills will pay dividends for many years to come, if not for your entire life.

The downside is that these skills take a long time to develop. An hour spent studying spelling today won't measurably boost your score on your science test tomorrow, even if you study words about science. Instead, it will pay off in tiny increments in various academic, workplace, and life situations over numerous years. As the hours you've spent studying add up, you'll start to see significant results in a wide variety of situations — but those hours will be hours that you didn't spend making the grades that show up on your report cards and transcripts.

Besides, as far as lifelong benefits are concerned, report cards and transcripts have their own rewards. In high school, better transcripts open the door to a better college education, and although you may forget within a week what you learned for your various tests, the improvements to your transcript will be immediate, noticeable, and permanent. Even in junior high or middle school, your classwork helps lay the foundation for future success in "sequential" subjects such as mathematics and (to a degree) the sciences. No matter what grade you're in, **study spelling only if you have time left over after keeping your classroom performance as high as you reasonably can.**

If the theory of "multiple intelligences" is correct, some people are very good at certain intellectual functions and less good at others. They may be only so good at math, for example, and beyond a certain point, no amount of extra studying will help them. If you fit this description — and be honest with yourself here, rather than looking for excuses — it may be OK to devote a lot of time to spelling even if your grades in certain other subjects could be better. To do so is just to acknowledge what economists call the law of diminishing returns: If all the extra study in that subject wouldn't help anyway, you might as well devote your efforts to other areas in which you can see results.

To summarize: **Because the benefits from competitive spelling accumulate slowly, if you need or want a quick boost to your grades, you are better off spending your time studying for the specific subjects in which you need improvement.**

2. **Legitimate but insufficient reasons to compete**: Taken by themselves, the following reasons aren't good enough to justify getting involved in the first place, but if you're already involved for the right reasons, these reasons provide good additional motivation.

   a. **Interacting with other people who love words and learning**

Higher levels of competition, especially nationals, provide excellent opportunities to meet and befriend people with whom you have a lot in common. If you're interested in competition for fundamentally sound reasons, meeting these people is a great side benefit. However, someone with no prior experience or track record has very slim chances of making it to nationals, and even regional competition lasts just one day. In terms of return on an investment, competitive spelling involves a lot of days sitting around reading books for a chance at a few days of meeting people. If meeting smart people who take learning seriously is your ultimate goal, spend your time on something more social that involves people closer to home, such as a trivia team or a debate, chess, or Scrabble club.

- It's possible to make spelling bee preparation something of a social event: You and your fellow competitors can get together, quiz each other, and share fun words and tips about languages you're learning. However, most students who live within traveling distance of one another will be competing against each other in local or regional bees. Because in-person group study also improves the skills of "the competition" and because co-championships are rare, few groups will gain much momentum, and even fewer will last beyond competition day.

  Of course, you can still stay friends with people after at least one of you no longer remains in competition. However, you can do the same with members of longer-lasting clubs that bring together people who see each other more frequently.

- Online study groups that bring together people from different regions can solve the problem of study groups' breaking up after a competition. Conceivably, such a group could last a whole competition year, from nationals one year to nationals the next. However, holding group meetings online greatly decreases or eliminates "face-to-face" social interaction, especially when group members are far enough away from each other that they cannot also meet in person.

b. **Academic and other public recognition**

1. For people in elementary and junior high school, the prospect of public recognition isn't a good reason to get started in competition, but it can be a good reason to *stay* involved in competition if you've given it a try for other reasons and discovered that you're good at it.

   a. Even if you have the intellectual aptitude necessary for success in spelling competition, figuring out that you have that aptitude involves investing enough time and effort to make success possible. In other words, even if your investment of time and effort will be a good one, you won't know that until you invest a substantial amount. From the perspective of someone who hasn't made that investment yet, there are other routes to success that promise you a better average return (on average, more recognition) on your investment.

   As mentioned before, your chances for placing high in competition are very slim when viewed from the perspective of someone at the outset, with no positive or negative track record. Unless you make it to nationals, few people

51

outside your home town or county will pay much attention. Unless you last well into the national finals, few people in your region will remember you once the next year's competition brings a new contestant. Only a solid finish at nationals will justify a mention on your college application, and only a very high finish (top five or so) will be worth noting in the "personal" section of your résumé as your career begins.

b. If you began competing for some other reason(s) and have found that you can do well, your situation is a bit different. Once you know that you can succeed – once your initial investment, made for some other reason(s), has brought you recognition as a side effect – you have some evidence that putting in additional time and effort will increase your rewards. Keep those other reasons in mind, especially if they're among the good ones that I discuss below, but it's OK to let the prospect of recognition motivate you once you have some evidence that you have what it takes to succeed.

2. If you are a recognition-seeking high schooler whose school participates in spelling competition (for example, Texas' UIL spelling and vocabulary division), go ahead and use any abilities and knowledge that you may have already developed, but exercise caution when investing additional time and energy.

High school students' time is much more valuable than that of younger students because of the other things that high school students could be doing with it. (Readers with an interest in economics may recognize the term "opportunity cost.") Most significantly, unlike middle or junior high school grades, high school grades count for the purpose of college admissions, and study time translates into grade points for even the smartest of students. Although success in extracurricular activities also matters, having better overall grades will count much more than will having success in one more extracurricular activity – especially when other people are using their time to improve their grades and compete against you for top spots in your class.

If you did well in junior high school, when your time was less precious, feel free to "recycle" the spelling skills that you developed then. In addition, go ahead and familiarize yourself with material that you know will figure prominently in your competition. (For example, in recent years, UIL has taken as many as 80% of its competition words from its "Word Power" study booklet.[11]) However, your time is now too valuable to speculate with it by seeking out, organizing, and studying large numbers of words not guaranteed to be of help.

This difference is magnified by the fact that if it's recognition you're looking for, the return on your investment in high school will be much less than it was or would have been in junior high: Where high school spelling competition exists at all, it has a much lower profile than do the elementary and junior high school competitions in the SNSB system, in part because there are so many other ways (most notably athletics) for high schoolers to gain recognition. In regions that don't participate in UIL or other competitions featuring high school spelling, people are unlikely to have heard of

---

[11] University Interscholastic League Constitution, 2007-08 edition, section 960(e).

them at all. College admissions officers may be more familiar with high school competitions, but remember that admissions officers also take into account how else you could have used your time.

Of course, if your success in earlier years was great enough that it continues to attract attention now, make a note of it when appropriate, such as in a college-admissions essay whose topic enables you to "sell" the benefits of your experience. (My discussion of my SNSB experience helped me get into Yale.)

In short, **if recognition is your goal, use the skills you have for what they're worth, but spend most of your time in high school doing other things, whether keeping your grades up or (if you're fortunate enough to have excellent grades already) diversifying your extracurricular portfolio.**

3. **Good reasons to compete**

    a. **Enjoyment of learning for its own sake**

        Perhaps you simply enjoy studying words and their origins. Perhaps you enjoy the more indirect learning that comes with the study of words: the knowledge that you gain about the fields in which those words are used. Either way, if you enjoy the process of preparation itself, you will find spelling bee competition rewarding no matter what level you reach or how high you place.

        Caution: Assuming that you're a student as most competitors are, I would repeat my previous warning to be sure that you're devoting enough attention to schoolwork – taking challenging courses and doing well in them –

before getting involved in competition. Even if you love all types of learning, **do the learning that you need to do before the learning that you want to do.** Competitive spelling is something to do with your spare time, time left over after you've gotten your grades in good shape and/or you've seen that putting more effort toward school study doesn't yield much improvement.

b. **Improvement of your memory and critical-thinking skills**

If you're preparing for competitive spelling in the right ways, both preparation and competition will help you become a better thinker in the ways discussed in Chapter II: "Book study" will develop your skills of memorization and of recognizing the general rules and patterns that govern the words that you encounter (induction). Conversely, spelling drills and actual competition will develop your skills of recalling what you have learned and of applying rules and patterns to words that you receive in competition (deduction). All four skills will serve you well long after you are finished with competitive spelling, whether in your education, in your career, or in your personal development.

Developing the thinking skills demanded by competitive spelling requires sustained effort over an extended period of time. If your purpose in developing them is to finish well in national competition, you will need to see something approaching full results by the time you reach eighth grade, the last year of eligibility for SNSB competition. For that reason, you will have to start early – fifth or sixth grade at the very latest – to develop these skills to the point where they can match those of other national competitors.

Even if you compete for only one year, however, serious effort can yield measurable improvement in these skills. If you're a student who enjoys learning, I encourage you to take part in competitive spelling even if you won't have the chance to catch up with your competitors in terms of experience and depth of knowledge. **By preparing for and competing in spelling bees, you can make yourself a better thinker and writer for the rest of your life, and achieving this goal is itself a victory.**

PART II: MAKING THE MOST OF YOUR TIME AND RESOURCES

In the abstract, preparation for spelling bees is a cycle with two phases: 1) finding words to study and 2) learning all that you can from those words by observing the elements that they have in common and the patterns that they follow. As you repeat this cycle and learn more words, the growth of the set of data that you have encountered will improve your ability to isolate word elements and observe patterns.

Of course, there's no need to focus entirely on one phase or the other at any given point in your preparation. There's no sense in passing up opportunities to notice new words just because you're currently using most of your study time to review words that you've already encountered. Likewise, it's good to keep your memory of previous words and patterns fresh even when your study consists mostly of learning new words. Besides, keeping yourself familiar with the patterns that you've learned will help you remember what to look for in new words, and keeping those patterns in mind will make it easier for you to revise them if you encounter examples inconsistent with them.

Below are the best word-finding and word-organization (*i.e.*, data-gathering and data-sorting) techniques that I've encountered to date. I've listed them in order of efficiency – in other words, in descending order of how well they *a*) introduce you to as many words as possible in a given amount of time and *b*) present those words in the way that enables you to notice their patterns as quickly and accurately as possible.

1: FINDING WORDS: A STARTING POINT FOR STUDY
WHERE TO FIND WORDS AND WORD ELEMENTS
THAT YOU ARE LIKELY TO ENCOUNTER IN COMPETITION

1. **"Keep your eyes open": Use the reading that you already do every day as an opportunity for spelling bee study.** Although other study techniques will introduce you to many more words than will this one taken in isolation, I've listed it first because it's at once the most time-efficient and probably the most personally rewarding way to prepare for spelling bee competition.

    All you need to do is *a*) **pay a bit closer attention to what you read or notice in print** and *b*) **make a note of unfamiliar or interesting words.** (It's a good idea to **keep a pencil and notepad with you at all times** so that you can look up these words and their definitions and etymologies later.) You will spend a little extra time here and there when going over what you read, but the improvement in your spelling will be significant. In fact, since the extra effort that this technique requires is so small, the returns on your time investment in it – the amount of help that it gives you per unit of time you spend – will likely exceed even the returns that you realize from studying competition word lists (also discussed below).

    What's more, paying closer attention to what you read will benefit you even when you aren't standing at the microphone.   Most obviously, when you pay closer attention to your reading, your comprehension of what you read – and with it your grades and standardized test scores – will improve.   In addition, by paying attention to the contexts in which you encounter different words and phrases, you will gain a greater appreciation of how writers use language for different purposes, and you will become a better writer and public speaker.

The following everyday activities are especially likely to bring you into contact with good "study words":

a. **Reading for classes in school:** As long as you're studying a subject for school, you might as well study two subjects at once, the second one being linguistics (and spelling in particular). Different subjects will help you learn different kinds of words and improve different aspects of your spelling ability. Here are some examples:

  i. Of all the subjects that you study, **science and mathematics** will introduce you to the most word elements that you are likely to encounter in spelling bees. The words that you encounter in junior high school textbooks will likely be a bit too familiar for regional and national competition, although you may encounter them at lower levels. However, the elements in those words will reappear in other combinations in less familiar words. A plurality of these elements will come from Greek, but almost as many will come from Latin, and you'll occasionally encounter German and French elements as well (especially in terms derived from proper names).

  Remember that when a foreign root enters English or the International Scientific Vocabulary (ISV),

English or the ISV will often alter the spelling of the word element that descends from that root. When it comes to knowing how an unfamiliar scientific term should look in print, a command of English scientific terminology is often even more helpful than is a direct familiarity with the foreign root(s) from which the English term is derived.

ii. It's obvious that studying the vocabulary of **foreign languages** will introduce you to roots from those languages. Less obvious is that when you study material in a foreign language, you have an opportunity to get a feel for the more general spelling or transliteration patterns that the language in question follows. In fact, these patterns are probably more important than any specific words (for spelling-bee purposes, read: roots) that you may learn in foreign-language courses.

At least at the junior high level, the words that you'll be learning are so basic that many of them will show up frequently as elements of English words that you're already studying. (Besides, the English words will reflect the changes that the foreign roots underwent as they entered English.)

In contrast, when you're up against a foreign "loan word" whose elements you've never seen or heard, your ability to apply the patterns that you've seen in its language of origin will be the only significant factor in whether or not you spell it correctly.

iii. **History and geography** provide valuable exposure to proper names and to eponyms, the common nouns and other everyday words that descend from proper names. History texts and other historical writings are probably the best sources of the personal names from which most eponyms are derived. Both historical writings and works dealing with geography will introduce you to place names that have lent themselves to everything from foodstuffs to minerals.

Think twice, however, before using a proper name as an example from which to draw a spelling rule or generalization for the language in which it arose. Proper names have often been around for a very long time, and their spellings do not shift over time as much as do the spellings of their respective languages' other words – meaning that the spelling of a proper name might not be a good example of the spelling or transliteration pattern that a language currently follows.

Proper names often represent "frozen forms," such as older spellings or regional variants, of words whose spellings changed or became uniform after a given proper name was adopted. Variations of this type are especially frequent in German names because of the numerous concerted efforts to reform German spelling and because those efforts have been concentrated within the years since Germany's political centralization in the late 1860s and early 1870s.

Conversely, if you are informed that a word is derived from a "name" or "geographic name," the word's spelling will depend on how the name of the relevant person (perhaps long dead) or location (perhaps in a region whose variety of the source language uses nonstandard spellings) is or was spelled – not on how the standard language would spell the name or how English would transliterate it according to the patterns used for that standard language today. For this reason, **rote memorization is the only way to learn some unusual proper names.**

On a side note, historical texts also occasionally feature legal or political terms related to the systems in place in the time period being discussed. These terms occasionally appear in study booklets and on national word lists.

iv. **Music and visual art** classes will introduce you to many technical terms used in their respective fields. Many or most terms that you encounter in class will be too common to be used in advanced competition. However, they're worth paying attention to for two reasons: First, even the easier terms are quite likely to show up in intermediate-level bees. Second, they are excellent examples from which to learn the orthographic patterns of their source languages (especially Italian for musical terms and French for visual-art terms).

v. Works of **literature**, especially classics of the English language, often feature characters whose names have been adopted as eponyms. Older works may feature words that remain part of the English language but do not describe objects or concepts found in everyday modern life. In this way, literary works can introduce you to words that you're unlikely to find in nonfiction texts describing the state of knowledge in a field as of when they were written. Finally, some English words are known primarily for their use in particular quotations, allusions, or time-worn stock phrases.

You may encounter those words in the literary passages that inspired the references that keep those words "alive" today.

vi. When you consult **reference materials** as you are doing research for a project or essay of any kind, an unfamiliar word – even one in an article that you are flipping past – may catch your eye. It's OK to be distracted by such a word, if only for a moment. Write it down and look it up when you reach a good stopping point in your research. (If you read reference materials for pleasure, keep a pencil and notepad with you as you would if you were studying.)

b. If your courses such as civics or social studies do not require you to read **newspapers**, I strongly advise that you do so in your spare time, both to improve your spelling and for your more general edification.

As far as spelling is concerned, newspapers will bring you words related to the latest developments in law, science, and medicine, along with the names of historical concepts and geographic locations that set the stage for current events. Although the names of persons involved in current events have usually not yet "made it into the dictionary," there are exceptions. Newspapers' discussions of the historical backgrounds of current controversies may introduce you to older personal names from which eponyms are derived.

A newspaper large enough to sponsor a regional competition usually features stories written in enough detail to bring you into contact with good words. (Subscribing to your sponsoring newspaper is also a small but meaningful way to say "thank you" to your sponsor!) Although the intellectual depth of major American news magazines has suffered in recent years, the United Kingdom's *Economist* is usually excellent — but because it follows British rather than American spelling conventions, be sure to check words that you encounter there against *Webster's Third* and, when differences exist, to remember which spelling is considered standard in which nation.

c. If you do other **pleasure reading**, keep pencil and notepad close at hand then as well. Keeping track of how many "good" words you encounter will give you a good indicator of how well you're challenging yourself with what you choose to read.

d. Be sure to keep track of technical terms that you encounter in your **extracurricular activities**. Some activities feature more specialized or unusual terms than others do — compare ballet or equestrianism against baseball — but no matter what activity you're involved in at any moment, don't pass up an opportunity to learn from it.

2. **Review lists of words that have been used in past national and regional competitions.** Whereas getting more out of your everyday reading is likely the most *efficient* way to study for spelling bees, this method is much more *effective* in absolute terms, *i.e.*, in terms of the sheer number of "good words" that you can learn by using it. Besides, it's highly efficient in its own right. In fact, **because this method of finding new words offers an unrivaled combination of efficacy with efficiency, past competitions' word lists are the overall-best type of word source. I therefore recommend that you devote to them a plurality – indeed, almost certainly even a**

majority – of the time that you spend gathering the **"raw data"** of new words.

Think of it this way: There's no better proof that a word could turn up in competition than the fact that it *has* turned up in competition. The same principle holds for the elements that make up those words: The more frequently an element is seen in words selected for use in competition, the more clear it is that the people selecting the words consider that element to be worth knowing. And when you're spending time on only words and elements that fit this description, the returns on your time investment can't be anything less than very good.

Lists of past "competition words" are available from a variety of sources:

- In 2003 and again in 2004, the SNSB released a free, online **Consolidated Word List** ("CWL") consisting of over 24,000 words used in past national competitions, along with definitions and etymologies for over 10,000 of those words. In late 2011 or early 2012, the SNSB deleted the downloadable CWL files from its servers, but not before the Internet Archive (http://www.archive.org/index.php) made copies and stored them on its own server. These copies are downloadable via http://wayback.archive.org/web/*/http://spellingbee.com/2003* (for 2003's version) and /2004* (for 2004's).[12]

---

[12] If clicking on a link in these pages directs you to a page containing a calendar, click on one of the dates highlighted using bold-faced text and/or colored circles. These dates are when the Internet Archive made and stored a copy of the page. If a given date's archive yields an error message or "not found"-type substitute page, visit an earlier date's archive, using the links in the calendar page's header to select a different year if necessary.

- **The SNSB's annually-published study booklet**, currently titled *Spell It!* but published in previous competition years under different formats titled *Paideia* (1995 through 2006) and *Words of the Champions* (1994 and earlier), contains words covering a variety of difficulty levels and subject matters. The SNSB does not offer previous years' study booklets for sale, but used copies are available at many online auction sites; prices vary with seasonal demand and with a given booklet's age and rarity.

- The SNSB's server used to retain **national competition round results** from competition years 2000 through 2007. The SNSB deleted these records in 2009, but the Internet Archive preserves copies of them as well. You can compile lists of words used in a given year and competition round by visiting http://web.archive.org/web/20091231235959/http://spellingbee.com/[last two digits of year]bee/rounds/Round[two digit round number].htm (for 2000-02 and 2004-07) or .shtml (for 2003), omitting brackets in each case.

- Some sponsors make available **previous years' Sponsor Bee Guides** – word lists used by many sponsors in regional competition – on a limited basis. For example, a sponsor may give Sponsor Bee Guides to the winner of its regional competition in order to help that winner prepare for nationals. Ask your sponsor to share these lists with you, but even if your sponsor says no, don't give up: If you or someone else in your family has ties to another sponsorship area known for helping its competitors or regional winner, you may be able to persuade someone in that sponsor's office to provide you copies of its old lists. (However, don't request or accept any help that you believe the employee to be prohibited from providing.)

- If you have befriended other spellers, consider asking them whether they have **past regional or national word lists** available.[13] Former spellers who retain a love for the competition are often willing or even eager to share their old materials. Online social-networking groups are particularly useful for finding and contacting spellers and former spellers who have access to old lists.

> *Tip:* Your odds of getting study materials from another currently active speller are better if you have something of your own to share in return.

> *Caution:* In most of these lists, words are arranged in order of difficulty rather than by their relationship to one another. This arrangement makes them good to use during competition drills when you're practicing for your time at the microphone, but it makes it hard to notice patterns followed by words from a given language and/or from a given root within that language. For the information-gathering phase of your preparation, save the definition, sentence, and etymological information provided in these lists, but rearrange the words and their accompanying information into a more useful format – more on that in "The 'Spelling Notebook'" below.

3. **Make judicious use of commercially available word lists.** Here, "judicious" has both quantitative and qualitative aspects. Quantitatively, these lists should constitute only a portion of your source material. Although

---

[13] Although it has long been common for national-level spellers to form study groups with their friends from previous years, during my time in competition I was not aware of the more specific practice of sharing word lists with fellow spellers. I first encountered that particular idea in *How to Spell Like a Champ* (*see* note 1 above).

their breadth and depth are often formidable, you mustn't assume that they are fully comprehensive, and you shouldn't rely on them to the exclusion of other sources. Qualitatively, you mustn't place unquestioning trust in the information that they do contain: That information can include entry-word spellings that contain typographical errors, definitions that are overly broad or narrow, and/or etymologies that are false or oversimplified. Moreover, even when you can find independent confirmation of a given piece of information, if that information is absent from *Webster's Third*, then SNSB judges will not verify it as correct, and if *Webster's Third* contradicts it, then the contrary information in *Webster's Third* will control.

That said, **the marketplace longevity and reputation of a commercially available list are generally reliable predictors of its quality.** Like all businesses, commercial list preparers have to think long-term, and the natures of their product and of their customer base give them even more incentive than usual to "get everything right the first time."

- The time that a list preparer's typical customer (*i.e.*, a contestant) spends in the market is at once *a*) short enough that preparers must engage in constant and large-scale outreach to new customers and *b*) long enough that retention of individual customers is important, especially given the relatively small size of this market niche.

- The potential consequences of a single mistake in a list are so disastrous that customers expect and demand absolute accuracy. Because the consequences of omitting useful words or information are not quite as severe, customers' expectations for completeness are not quite as high as those for accuracy. However, between the number of sellers in the market and the limitations on many buyers' resources, preparers face high competitive pressure to make their lists extremely comprehensive while not diluting and "bloating" them with too-easy words.

- Serious competitors' emotional attachment to competition strengthens the loyalty with which they reward good help and the grudges that they bear if they are led astray, often to the point that one attitude or the other far outlasts its bearer's eligibility for competition. Many past contestants are eager to give advice about which sources to study and which to avoid, and many current competitors are just as eager to listen.

- Finally, the close knit of the competitive-spelling community has long done to list preparers' business models what the rise of online social media has more recently done to commerce as a whole: It multiplies the speed with which opinions travel and reputations change, severely limiting preparers' ability to rest on past successes and/or escape notice of recent stumbles.

By extension, these factors also predict fairly well the quality of other study materials produced by the same author(s), who likely exercised similar diligence in preparing their other works, and/or released by the same publisher, which likely applies similar quality-control standards and procedures to its other titles.[14]

According to the above standards, and as my own competition experience confirms, **by far the best**

---

[14] This second correlation is especially strong if a list's preparers self-publish it or operate the company that publishes it: In such a case, their initial diligence and their subsequent quality control are different manifestations of a single underlying variable.

commercially available study list is Hexco Academic's *Nat's Notes,* revised and expanded under the title *New Nat's Notes.* Named for one of the three SNSB-veteran sisters whose family operates Hexco, this list is designed for experienced competitors; most words appearing on it are difficult or extremely difficult. In mid-2012, Hexco released a newly revised edition of *New Nat's Notes (NNN)*; until then, the edition released in February 2007 had been most recent. *NNN* and other Hexco products are available for purchase online at http://www.hexco.com.

- *NNN* contains definitions and brief etymologies for all of its more than 18,000 words. (Hexco counted 19,159 list entries in *NNN*'s 2007 edition but publicized only this more general figure during the 2012 release.)

- *NNN* is available in two versions: one that lists its words alphabetically and one that arranges the same set of words in random order. (The randomly ordered version replaces the 2007 edition's version ordered by word length, a rough – albeit only rough – proxy for word difficulty.) I recommend the randomly ordered version because its structure suits it better for use in competition drills (see page 72 below).

- Four of the six SNSB national champions who won between *NNN*'s 2007 and 2012 releases used *NNN* in their study, as did all six runners-up.[15]

NNN's few weaknesses include *a*) Hexco's longstanding reliance on an oversimplified diacritical system that obscures some phonetic and syllabic distinctions and *b*) the

---

[15] Hexco provided these statistics, but I consider them unbiased and reliable, in part because *a*) their traceability to specific individuals makes them readily verifiable and *b*) Hexco's heavy use of them in its publicity has made them available to a wide audience of potential fact-checkers.

compilation's high price ($175.00 for *NNN*'s 2012 edition). Even these flaws, however, are as minor as they are few: The first one amounts to "room for improvement" in future editions, and as for the second, the breadth and depth of *NNN*'s assistance make it well worth even that substantial investment.

4. **Look through dictionaries and glossaries specific to particular fields in which many useful words and word elements appear.**

Dictionaries of medical terms are the best-known examples of this type of reference book. When preparing for my second and third trips to nationals, I used *Taber's Medical Word Book with Pronunciations*[16], which introduces you to each specific root by giving its definition, its origin, and examples of terms involving it. These example words are often good starting points for a "spelling notebook" entry (see section 2 below) dealing with the root that they illustrate.

While legal terminology occurs somewhat less frequently in competition than does medical terminology, **legal dictionaries** can also be quite helpful. Among legal dictionaries, *Black's Law Dictionary*[17] is the most famous, the most comprehensive, and (perhaps for these reasons) among the most expensive. Look for a used copy; online stores often feature the best prices.

---

[16] Clayton L. Thomas (editor), Philadelphia: F. A. Davis & Co., 1990, ISBN-13 #978-0-8036-8265-9.

[17] Bryan A. Garner (editor), St. Paul, Minn.: West Group, 2004, ISBN-13 #978-0-3141-5199-0. I did not use *Black's* during my preparation for competition because I did not encounter it until ten years too late, during my first year of law school. As soon as I noticed the school library's copy and began thumbing through it, however, I realized that I would have benefited from reviewing it while preparing for competition.

Dictionaries from other fields, such as many of the applied and pure sciences, are also available.

Caution: Technical dictionaries are great for learning foreign roots and English elements, but if you use them to encounter specific words, be sure to check those words' spellings in *Webster's Third* before studying them further. *Webster's Third* is the dictionary that the SNSB uses to determine whether a spelling is correct or incorrect, and a spelling listed as correct in your technical dictionary may not appear in *Webster's Third*.

Caution regarding the study of word lists and dictionaries

Let the collection of words from pre-prepared word lists and technical dictionaries be a starting point for your preparation rather than your main study technique. Although simply reading through these compilations will give you some help in memorizing elements and recognizing patterns, there are more efficient ways to use your time than poring over the same source material time and time again, regardless of that source material's quality.

In lists prepared for use by competition officials, similar words are not grouped together and may even be intentionally kept apart. In dictionaries, the typical alphabetical arrangement of words has the effect that a prefix is often the only element (if any) that words near each other have in common. It's a lot easier to notice patterns governing words with similar roots and languages of origin, especially "higher-order" patterns ("patterns of patterns"), when those words are kept together for ready comparison. In turn, making patterns more noticeable in this way makes it a lot easier to contrast different languages' spelling or transliteration patterns.

Instead of reading prepared lists over and over, go through them just once: Arrange the words from these lists into your own master list, putting each word – accompanied by its definition and its etymology – in a group with other words sharing the same root, language of origin, and/or subject matter. (Computers make this task much easier; see "The 'Spelling Notebook'" below for more specific ideas on how to compile this master list.)

> *Tip:* After your initial pass through a pre-prepared word list, especially one designed to be used in competition, put it aside and save it for "competition drills" in which a partner acts as pronouncer/judge and you ask questions and spell as you would in competition. This is one setting in which it's *good* to keep similar words separate from one another: By reducing the influence of recently reviewed words on your thought process, separating similar words improves your practice and refines your testing of long-term memory and abstract analogy.

For these reasons, the worst widely-used study method is the one that (quite unfortunately) first comes to mind in popular imagination: sitting down in front of an unabridged dictionary and reading it cover to cover. **The unabridged dictionary is the ultimate word list, and the pitfalls of word-list study are at their most severe when the list is the dictionary itself.** Words that share elements (other than prefixes), language(s) of origin, and/or subject matter are scattered across the unabridged dictionary's thousands of pages, making it as hard as possible to notice the patterns that they follow. Common words without useful elements waste your time if you study them and break your momentum if you skip over them.

Moreover, the sheer magnitude of this task is likely to discourage you from both it and other studying. If you *do* complete a comprehensive study of the unabridged dictionary itself, you are likely to have spent an unhealthy amount of time doing so and to have paid too little attention to other forms of study, schoolwork, and your social life.

> *Tip:* Even if you have an eidetic or "photographic" memory, arranging words so that you can notice their patterns will help you if you're asked to spell a word that you overlooked in the first place. For example, better attention to patterns might have helped one speller against whom I competed in 1994: Although he had memorized the entire main section of the unabridged dictionary, he missed a word, likely of Italian origin, that was taken from the Addenda Section, which he had not studied.

This isn't to say that you should throw the unabridged dictionary out the window (figuratively or literally). Instead, keep it close at hand, but make consulting it the *second* step in your study process, using it to get complete and "official" information about words that you've encountered elsewhere.

If you feel compelled to study straight from the unabridged dictionary, do so by skimming it, stopping to make note of a word only when it or one of its elements gets your attention as being unfamiliar. When you get a fair number of these words, take a break to add each word, its definition, and its etymology to your master list in the proper place or places. After you're done – or after the dictionary is done with you – devote the bulk of your study time to your master list. You can then better notice patterns governing the words that you've studied and learn the elements and roots that appear in those words.

Again, to learn everything possible from the words that you encounter, you need to do more than just keep a running list of them and stare at it hour after hour. You need to review your "study words" systematically, comparing and contrasting them with one another. To notice as many patterns and learn as many roots as possible, you need to **study groups of words with similar origins and related meanings.**

It's true that some commercially prepared word lists (see item 3 of the previous section) feature some efforts at organization by etymology and/or meaning. However, for helping you learn to observe spelling patterns and determine which patterns an unfamiliar word follows, **there's no substitute for putting together the evidence yourself.** Even if a list comes "pre-organized," you need to pay close attention to each of its entries, analyzing each word in light of its associated information as you incorporate its entry into your overall list – and using *Webster's Third* to check that information and to look up and fill in anything missing.

Most top finishers at nationals maintain a "spelling notebook," a paper and/or electronic collection of words to study and of rules or generalizations to follow if they're given words that they haven't studied. Although spellers, parents, and coaches have been preparing notebooks for years, the SNSB began officially encouraging this practice in the late 1990s, when Carolyn Andrews, then an educational consultant for the SNSB and later its word list manager, started giving tips for notebook organization in her online column *Carolyn's Corner.* [18, 19]

---

[18] *See, e.g.*, http://web.archive.org/web/20080522074633/http://www.spellingbee.com/glance/organized.shtml.

- Although the SNSB discontinued this valuable study resource after the 2008 national finals and has removed the associated pages from its website, the Internet Archive proves its worth yet again by storing numerous installments of the column.[20]

Suggested notebook structure and compilation procedure

In my opinion, **a good starting point for organizing a spelling notebook is to create what amount to two parallel versions of the same word list:** *a*) **a version fundamentally organized by the language of origin of your list's words and**, if time permits, *b*) **a version fundamentally organized by the respective subject matters to which those words relate.** Each word, definition, and etymology that you encounter and put in your notebook will therefore appear at least twice: at least once in your notebook's language-of-origin section and at least once in its subject-matter section.

My recommendation to maintain a "subject-matter-first" version of your list was inspired by the structure of *Paideia*, the

---

[19] Carolyn Andrews is my mother and was my main coach during my competing years. (Thanks, Mom!) After I won the 1994 national competition, Bee officials learned that she had been my coach and had taught English and worked as a technical editor for several years, and they offered her a position.

[20] *See* http://web.archive.org/web/20091231235959/http://spellingbee. com/cc[two-digit year number: 97 through 09]/week[two-digit week number: see below]/cchome.htm (for competition years 1997 through 1999) or /cchome.shtml (for competition years 2000 through 2009), omitting brackets in each case. Unfortunately, the pages for many weeks of most competition years, especially late in a given year, are either incompletely archived or entirely absent. The last fully stable sets of archived pages are those of Week 17 for 1997, 36 for 1998, 13 for 1999, 23 for 2000, 33 for 2001, 27 for 2002, 32 for 2003, 31 for 2004, 33 for 2005, 34 for 2006, 18 for 2007, 22 for 2008, and 07 for 2009, although some subsequent weeks' archives (especially from later years) contain some accessible content.

SNSB's official study guide during competition years 1995 through 2006. Although I'm not sure what factors motivated the SNSB to switch to subject-matter-based categorization (or away from it, for that matter), I have two reasons for recommending this parallel method as a supplement to your etymology-focused efforts:

1. Grouping words by subject on your study list helps organize words and their elements in your mind as well. By increasing the number of different ways in which your overall list is organized, you can make your notebook reflect an increased number of independent, qualitatively different relationships that those words have to each other. Once you lay this groundwork and follow through by diligently studying your different "sub-lists," the mental processes of association (described in Chapter II's discussion of recollection) and "chunking" (described in Chapter I's discussion of requests for a word's use in a sentence) will take over, creating new ways for your mind to access each of your "study words" if and when you're called on to spell it or a word sharing one or more of its elements.

2. Grouping words by subject enables you to study a subject while you're studying the words that deal with it. Increasing the proximity of words related to a given subject will improve the focus of your learning about that subject as you read through your notebook. You'll then be able to remember what you've learned more as a coherent body of knowledge and less as a bunch of unassociated facts.

If you're on a tight preparation schedule and don't have time to update two versions of the same set of words at once, the "subject-matter-first" half of the notebook is the one to dispense with. If you have time, however, its benefits are worth the added investment.

1. **Compile a master list of the "study words" that you have encountered so far.** At least in conceptual terms, the first step in compiling a spelling notebook is what you might expect: to **gather all the word information you've encountered** – whether it's jotted down on notebook or scrap paper, commercially printed in one or more word lists that you've acquired, or saved electronically in a list that you've already begun compiling – **in a single place.**

    The next step is to **place all of your "study words" on a single list, making sure to keep each word together with any associated definition or etymological information** that you may have collected.

    - If you have access to a **computer with word-processing, database, and/or spreadsheet software**, I strongly recommend that you **use it from the very start of this process (and make regular backups of your work!)**: The tasks that you'll be performing – including but not limited to creating, editing, sorting, and duplicating the entries on your list – will be arduous enough even with a computer's help, and without it they will be nearly impossible.

        - Using software of one of these types will allow you to improve your notebook's organization dramatically: Rather than simply adding words and their definitions at the end of the categories and sub-categories in which they belong, you'll be able to insert them at the most appropriate places within those lists, improving your mental organization of *all* the words that you study. Moreover, because *a)* you won't need to leave excess space at the end of each category and *b)* you can remove page breaks where it won't hurt to do so, you can make your notebook a lot more physically streamlined and a lot easier to carry around!

- **"Copy and paste" is your friend.** Just as editing within your notebook keeps it tightly organized, copying and pasting enables you to make efficient use of your study time: When you're starting an entry for a new word element, "Control+F" (or whatever you use as a "find" command) will help you find any words containing that element that are already in your notebook. You can then just copy them from one place and paste them into another rather than laboring with pencil and paper.

  Copying and pasting can also help you even earlier in the process: If you can afford it, it's probably worth the expense to **purchase a CD-ROM of the latest unabridged edition of _Webster's New International Dictionary_.** After you notice words in print and make a quick note of them, you can return to your computer, look them up, and **copy and paste their definitions and etymologies alongside them.**

As you're compiling this list, it's a good idea to **put each "study word" in boldface or otherwise set it apart from the information that follows it.** Doing so makes the word easier to notice and identifies it on both a conscious and a subconscious level as the "raw material" on which your skills of pattern recognition should operate.

It's probably best to **start the compilation process by focusing on one or a few of your sources.** I recommend this approach for two reasons:

a. Depending on which source(s) you select, narrowing your initial focus may improve your future ability to focus on the sources that remain, making the compilation process more efficient throughout. For example, if you begin by typing out your handwritten notes, then by getting those random pieces of paper out of the way, you'll save yourself the time and energy that you'd otherwise spend preventing them from getting "lost in the shuffle" during your work with other sources.[21]

b. What's more, the initial success of producing something tangible and immediately useful will likely boost your confidence in your ability to finish the job. By contrast, if you don't break down the compilation process into manageable units, the prospect of listing all of the words from all of your sources will seem even more daunting, than it otherwise would.

To give yourself a sense of your notebook's structure, it's helpful to **ensure that your initial selection of source(s) covers a wide variety of material:** numerous languages of origin (the more distantly related, the better), numerous roots within each of those languages, and preferably a broad range of subject matter. Doing so enables you to get an early start on setting up the framework of categories and sub-categories into which you'll sort your words (more on that in a moment), with the effect that from the outset (or close) you'll have a good grasp of what your notebook will eventually look like.

---

[21] Paper copies do provide some degree of independent backup, albeit an inefficient one, in case some kind of catastrophe destroys your computerized list and all of its electronic backups. For this reason, I recommend that in an abundance of caution you **store your handwritten originals somewhere convenient** rather than discarding them.

Once you finish with a given source, it wouldn't hurt to **put the words from that source in alphabetical order**, again keeping each word together with its definition and etymological information. You'll eventually need to alphabetize the words anyway (again, more on that in a moment), and it's more efficient to alphabetize the overall list at a single (key)stroke than it would be to sort all your words and then have to alphabetize every single category-within-a-category.

Finally, to prepare for the sorting process below, **create a dividing line or other indicator to separate words that you've already begun sorting from words that you haven't.** As you enter additional words and their information into your master list, be sure that you're putting them in the "not-yet-sorted" section!

2. Next, **go through your master list word by word. Look up each word in** *Webster's Third.*

   - **If you cannot find a given word (as spelled on your list) in** *Webster's Third* **and if you are using an electronic version, see whether the software suggests any alternative spellings.**

     - **If it does, investigate the suggestions and see whether any of them match(es) any other information that you have.**

       - **If *a*) only one suggestion matches any of your definitions and/or etymological information *or b*) all listed suggestions are variants of each other:** Chances are that you copied the word incorrectly or that it was misspelled in your source material. **Remove and discard the spelling in your master-list** entry and replace that spelling with the spelling(s) in *Webster's Third*.

- **If *a*) different suggestions match different pieces of information *and b*) at least two of those suggestions are not variants of each other:** You have probably confused or conflated two or more separate words. **Create a separate entry for each suggestion,** keeping together any suggestions that are variants of each other, **and move each piece of information to the entry in which it belongs.**

- **If a given piece of information does not match any suggestions:** It may belong to a word not on the suggestion list, it may relate to a usage that *Webster's Third* does not recognize as standard, or your source may have included it in error. **"Copy and paste" the spelling in your entry, any suggested alternative spellings, and the non-matching information into a separate file listing dubious information to investigate later.** Then **remove the non-matching information from your master list.**

- **If *Webster's Third* does not suggest any alternative spellings, remove the master-list entry entirely by "cutting and pasting" it into the dubious-information file mentioned above.**

- If *Webster's Third* does confirm a given word's spelling as correct, **check against the *Webster's Third* entry any other information that you have. Remove any information inconsistent with the information in**

Webster's Third and "flag" as possibly incorrect any information that *Webster's Third* neither contradicts nor confirms. Then **copy onto your list any definition(s) and/or etymological information** present in *Webster's Third* but until now absent from your list.

3. Once you've compiled and checked your master list (or a subset consisting of the words from certain sources), **sort your words by language of origin.**

At this point, I recommend that you **create a new file separate from your master list.** This way, you can "copy and paste" from your master list rather than altering the master list itself.

Once you've created the new file, **divide it into language-of-origin sections.** In your electronic file, I recommend using a **page break**, along with a section break if your software supports that feature. When you print out your list, I recommend adding a **notebook divider** at the corresponding point.

It's good to start by **creating a section for each language that you know will be among your words' languages of origin.** Perhaps that language is among the "usual suspects" frequently encountered in competition – including but not limited to Latin, Greek, French, German, Italian, Spanish, Old English, Japanese, and the Polynesian languages (including Hawaiian) – or perhaps you happen to recall seeing that language in the etymology section of one or more entries on your master list.

In any event, you don't need to spend a great deal of time "up front" on this task: You don't need a section for every language that's ever existed. Indeed, you don't even need

82

to start with a comprehensive list of all the languages represented in your master word list – **if at any point you encounter a language of origin for which you don't yet have a section, simply start a new section at the appropriate point in your list.**

Where that point is depends on the order in which you place the various categories that you create. **Arrange your language-of-origin categories** – whether created initially or added later – **according to whatever method works best for you.**

- If you naturally tend to arrange your knowledge into conceptual hierarchies, then you might order your categories "genealogically" or "taxonomically" by language family, sub-family, and so forth.

- If visual learning is your strongest suit, then you might order your categories geographically by continent and then by latitude or longitude of the region where each language was first spoken.

- If you're the pragmatic type, then you might arrange your categories in descending order of how often their respective languages appear in competition[22] or, more simply, in alphabetical order by language name.

Once a word's master-list entry reflects all the information in *Webster's Third* and does not contradict any of it, **"copy and paste" the word's master-list entry into each**

---

[22] Frequency data averaged across the SNSB's 2008, 2011, and 2012 nationals appear throughout the third edition of Scott Remer's *Words of Wisdom: Keys to Success in the Scripps National Spelling Bee* (Charleston, S.C.: CreateSpace, 2014, ISBN-13 #978-1-4949-3694-5), edited by Erica Remer.

section corresponding to a language of origin from which the word is derived.

- If different parts of a word have different languages of origin, be sure to paste the word (in its entirety) into the section for each of those languages. At the same time, however, be sure to **indicate which part of the word is from a given section's language** so that you will know which part is evidence of the spelling patterns that govern that language – and so that the other parts of the word won't confuse you when you're trying to figure out how that language looks on paper. For example, along with putting the entirety of each "study word" in boldface to set it apart from its accompanying information, I recommend underlining those and only those portions that are derived from the language into whose section you are pasting it.

Once you've completed this process for a given word, **go back to your master list and move that word's entry** (the one that you just "copied and pasted") **from your master list's "not-yet-sorted" section to its "already-sorted" section.** It's true that you haven't finished the sorting process for that word, but what's important is that you've copied the word to the new list. The new list will contain its own indicators of how much further a given word needs to be sorted.

4. **Within each language-of-origin section, sort that section's words by** *a)* **creating a subsection corresponding to each root or element that you encounter,** *b)* **"copying and pasting" each word's entry into each subsection corresponding to one of the word's roots in the given language, and then** *c)* **removing the entry from the broader language-of-origin section,** with the net effect that the word now

84

appears in (and only in) each subsection that corresponds to one of its roots.

Note: *This recommendation represents a change from my advice in early printings of this guide. See the end of this section for details.*

As with the broader language-of-origin sections, **it's good to have a clear division between root/element subsections**, although the separation shouldn't be as great. Staying on the same page, skipping two or three lines, and creating a **centered heading featuring the root** (preferably in boldface and/or italics) **and its meaning** (preferably in quotation marks) should be enough.

It's probably best to list root/element subsections in alphabetical order of their spelling (if their language of origin uses the Roman alphabet) or of their transliteration according to the most widely accepted system for their language of origin (if it does not use the Roman alphabet).

5. **Within each root/element subsection, arrange your "study words" alphabetically, again being sure to keep each word together with its definition(s) and etymological information.** Doing so will make it easier for you to locate a specific word if you have that word on your mind and wish to review its information.

6. Now that you have fully sorted your "study words," **return to each language-of-origin category and create at its beginning a section for listing spelling/transliteration rules and patterns that this language obeys.** The more uniformly a language of origin follows certain patterns, the more important it is to have those patterns in your notebook for review. (Hawaiian and Japanese are good examples of highly rule-governed languages of origin.)

It's all right if at this point you've made few or no observations appropriate for these sections; you'll **add and revise them over the course of your study.** (Of course, if you *have* already observed some rules and/or patterns, you should go ahead and add them.) As you begin and maintain each language's list, I recommend that you **arrange these rules and patterns in descending order of their scope:** Begin with those that apply to all or most words derived from that language, and end with those that apply only in highly specific situations such as *a*) before or after a certain letter/sound or *b*) in a certain grammatical situation.

Once you've used the above procedure to sort all your words, **your list will have the following structure:**

I. **Set of all words that are worth studying (master list)**

    A. **Set of words having a given language of origin** ("first-order" division), with languages of origin ordered according to whatever system you chose during step 3 above

        1. **List of spelling/transliteration rules governing this language,** arranged from most generally applicable to most situation-specific

        2. **Set of words derived from a specific root in this language or containing a specific element adapted from that root** ("second-order" division), with root elements presented in alphabetical order as spelled (if language uses Roman alphabet) or as transliterated according to most widely accepted system (if language does not use Roman alphabet)

            a. **Specific word derived from the root in question or containing an element adapted from it,** with these words presented in alphabetical order: This is technically a "third-order" division, but you don't need a formal heading corresponding to each word; the word itself is enough of a divider, especially if you emphasize it as I describe below.

i. **Word's spelling**, *i.e.*, word as it appears in print: I recommend that you *a*) set apart and emphasize the word by placing it in boldface and *b*) further emphasize any and all roots/elements from the present language-of-origin category by underlining them.

ii. **Word's definition(s)**, listed in the order in which they appear in *Webster's Third*

iii. **Etymological information about all parts of the word**, preferably in the beginning-to-end order found in *Webster's Third*: Because your "second-order" section heading has already provided this information for the root or element in whose category this instance of the word appears, you can probably condense your notebook a bit by leaving it out.

If you follow these guidelines when putting words into your notebook, then when you review that notebook you will be able to familiarize yourself with both a language's roots and its spelling patterns at the same time.

Compilation procedure for list organized by words' subject matter

1. **Develop an initial list of subject-matter categories.** Once you've compiled your "etymology-first" study list, you'll have a good idea of what subjects appear frequently in its words' definitions. If you need further suggestions, see the list in the step below.

2. As with languages of origin in your notebook section focused on etymology, **arrange your subject-matter categories using whatever method your mind naturally uses for organizing the information in those categories.**

   For example, your categories might proceed in order from "most real" to "most ideal":

   - "What couldn't be otherwise" (logic and mathematics)

   - "What must be and what can be in our world as it is" (physics, chemistry, biology/medicine, and technology)

   - "What behavior and decision patterns humans tend to exhibit" (psychology, economics, sociology, and descriptive political science and legal theory)

   - "Which among the set of possible behaviors and decisions specific individuals have chosen" (history)

   - "Which possible outcomes people ought to choose" (ethics and normative political and legal philosophy)

   - "What it would be supererogatory [*i.e.*, 'above and beyond the call of duty'] for people to choose" (aesthetics, including the visual, musical, and culinary arts)

   - "What couldn't possibly, can't, doesn't, and/or didn't happen" (fictional literature)

3. Once you've arranged your subject-matter categories into a sensible order, **"copy and paste" the words and accompanying information from your master list into the appropriate category or categories.** Again, if a word deals with multiple subject matters, paste it into multiple categories. As you're copying and pasting, it's a good idea to **check each word's entry for alternate definitions** so

that you can make sure to paste your word into those definitions' subject-matter categories.

4. After sorting the words on your master list into the categories that you've chosen, you should use the procedure described in the "etymology-first" section to

   a) **subdivide each subject-matter category by language of origin,** preferably arranging language divisions in the same order used above;

   b) **further divide each language sub-category by specific root/element,** preferably arranging roots/elements alphabetically; and then

   c) **transfer a copy of each word's entry into each root/element category corresponding to part of that word,** preferably *i)* arranging entries in their words' alphabetical order and *ii)* indicating which portion or portions of a word correspond to the language sub-category within which you're working.

   Once you've done so, even this half of your notebook will preserve the benefits of etymological grouping to at least some degree.

Using subject matter as your initial basis for word sorting does have two drawbacks:

1. If you start with subject matter, then you can't sort words by language of origin until later in the process. As a result, starting with subject matter has the effect of scattering words having the same language of origin (and often even words sharing roots or elements) across different subject-matter categories, limiting your ability to recognize and memorize patterns as you study.

Fortunately, maintaining a parallel "etymology-first" version of your master list will offset this limitation.

2. Because each subject-matter category will require its own language-of-origin subdivisions, the number of language categories that you need to create will in theory be multiplied by the number of subject-matter categories that your list features. The only exceptions in practice will occur when your study of a given subject matter hasn't yet brought you into contact with any words from a given language.

As a result, you shouldn't begin each language-of-origin division with a list of all the spelling/transliteration rules governing that division's language: Doing so would require you to reprint that entire list in each subject-matter category containing even one word from the corresponding language. In addition to bloating the "subject-matter-first" half of your notebook, this redundancy would break both your overall concentration and your focus on the subject matter as you attempt to study. In the process, it would largely defeat the purpose of your adding the "subject-matter-first" half to begin with.

Instead, you'll need to make an additional change in the format of the "subject-matter-first" half of your notebook: **Concentrate your various language-rule lists in a separate section at the start of this half of your notebook.** Doing so enables you to **briefly review all of your observations so far about all languages that you've studied to date** before turning your attention to a given subject that may well feature words from many or all of these languages.

If you follow the above recommendations, **the second half of your notebook will have the following structure:**

II. **"Subject-matter-first" section of notebook**

    A. **Comprehensive list of spelling and/or transliteration rules, sorted by language of origin** to whose words a given rule applies

        1. **Language-specific rule list** (1 for each language), with language-specific lists arranged according to whatever system you chose in step 3 of compiling your etymology-focused section

            a. **Rule** (1 entry for each), with rule entries arranged in descending order of scope (see step 6 of the recommended procedure for compiling your etymology-focused section)

    B. **"Master list" of words**, this time **arranged by subject matter**

        1. **Words dealing with a given subject matter** (1 section per subject), with subject-matter sections arranged however works best for you

            a. **Words dealing with this subject matter AND having a given language of origin**: 1 subsection per language, with languages arranged in the same order method as in I.A and II.A.1 above

                i. **Words dealing with this subject matter and derived from a specific root in this language** (see I.A.2 for details)

                    (a) **Specific word derived from the root in question or containing an element adapted from it** (see I.A.2.a)

                        (1) **Word's spelling** (see I.A.2.a.i)

(2) **Word's definition(s)** (see I.A.2.a.ii)

(3) **Word's etymological information** (see I.A.2.a.iii)

See Appendix B for a condensed overall outline of a study notebook organized according to the above principles.

Of course, organizing your words by language of origin and subject matter is just a starting point: You will likely want to **add "specialty sections"** – or perhaps even start a "specialty notebook" – **dealing with specific, frequently occurring problems** such as being asked to decide between *-able* and *-ible* or between *-ant* and *-ent*. For each section, be sure to make a note of the general rules and patterns that you observe — and be sure to accompany each generalization with a list of specific examples and a list of exceptions.

Explanation of change in recommendation regarding list organization

In early printings of this guide, I recommended that competitors divide each language-of-origin section into subsections each dealing with a specific subject matter and *then* divide those subsections into "third-order" sections corresponding to individual roots. I've since had second thoughts about that recommendation:

- First, when divisions by subject matter occur within other divisions, the subject matter that you're studying will shift more frequently than it would if subject matter determined the "first-order" divisions of your list as a whole. As a result, you'll realize only a fraction of the benefits that come from studying groups of words whose common bond is their meaning (as opposed to their etymology). This reduction becomes even more severe as the level at which you place your subject-matter divisions becomes "deeper": If you attempt to keep words with shared etymologies together by placing your subject-matter divisions within the subsection for a given root/element, then many subject-matter divisions will contain only one or a few words.

- Second, you can still realize those benefits by adopting my continuing recommendation that you create a second, parallel organization of your master list in which subject matter *is* the initial criterion by which you sort your "study words."

- Third, the costs of adding the subject-matter "tier" to this portion of your notebook are substantial:

  - The additional tier adds another layer of complexity that you'll have to sift through both when adding words and when reviewing them.

  - When division by subject matter precedes division by root or element (as it did in my earlier recommendation), words sharing a given root or element are scattered across subject matters, largely defeating the purpose of the "etymology-first" section of the notebook.

Therefore, my current inclination is to retract my earlier recommendation on this point and instead advise that you should **omit any consideration of subject matter from the "etymology-first" section of your notebook, saving subject matter for a separate, parallel section in which it is the primary criterion for organizing your list.**

3(?): "The Coaching Question"

If you join or visit an Internet discussion group devoted to competitive spelling, chances are that in very short order you will encounter one or more lively discussions about whether financially able families of one or more extremely serious competitors should hire a professional academic coach or tutor to assist their speller(s) on an individual basis. (When the national finals are in progress, the lobbies of the competition site are home to equally animated in-person discussions.) Some families swear by professional coaching; others shake their heads and laugh at the concept.

For what it's worth, here's my take: **I strongly discourage the use of professional coaching unless all available alternatives have become clearly inefficient uses of time** – a situation that is unlikely to arise for the vast majority of even the most talented and serious competitors. (See below for examples of available alternatives.) Studying with a professional coach is analogous to studying straight from the unabridged dictionary: Neither offers much, if any, improvement over the next-best alternative (to a professional coach, the alternatives listed below; to the dictionary, competition word lists) — and both demand resources (parents' money and a competitor's time, respectively) far disproportionate to the benefits that they provide.

Before even thinking about finding and hiring a professional coach, make sure to get everything you can out of the following alternatives (along with any others that you can think of):

1. If a student's **parents** have the time to work with the student, and especially if they have background knowledge and reasoning skills of the type that successful competitors exhibit (see Part II), they will be the helpers most accessible in the short term, most able to maintain a relationship over the long term, and most dedicated to the student's development over the duration.

2. As mentioned in Part I's discussion of opportunities to interact with other language enthusiasts, the rise of **online**

social networking has enabled students to help each other practice regardless of their respective geographic locations, greatly reducing what were formerly the two greatest barriers to mutual assistance, namely *a*) the diffusion of a small number of serious competitors over a wide area and *b*) the fact that any competitors who *are* able to meet in person will likely face each other at the school, local, or regional level, such that cooperation would reduce each participant's chances of advancing almost as much as it would improve them.

It is true that even long-distance collaborators will face the latter obstacle if multiple members of a given group advance to nationals. However, other factors unique to the long-distance scenario make the effort worthwhile. These factors include the improvement of long-distance collaborators' chances against other well-prepared national finalists, the prestige of even making it to nationals (and thus the rationality of a "risk-averse" strategy), and the still-substantial likelihood that one collaborator or another will be eliminated before then.

3. If a student already receives tutoring or academic coaching that follows a more general program, and if the tutor has already proven capable and reliable over time, **integrating spelling and language study into the student's existing tutoring program** can offer the benefits specific to trained assistance while avoiding the drawbacks (discussed below) associated with finding and hiring an academic coach for spelling-bee preparation alone.

4. A student's **local community** likely features at least a few kind souls who enjoy language arts and are willing to **volunteer one-on-one help**. Community members likely to fit the bill include **teachers, high-achieving older students** (including any **former high-level competitors**

who still live nearby), and **peers who are academically inclined but who are not themselves interested in competing.**

■ Under many circumstances, parents may find it appropriate to reward an unpaid one-on-one assistant, especially an older student, with gifts or small amounts of spending money intended as tokens of appreciation rather than as any kind of compensation. Even when parents do so, the unpaid assistant remains better characterized as a volunteer – a person acting from charitable motives rather than pursuing a means to earn money – and work with him or her will provide the advantages (discussed below) unique to volunteer assistance.

Contrary to what one might expect, **the help of a knowledgeable and caring volunteer will likely be as good as or better than the help that a typical paid tutor would provide.** Although this claim seems to fly in the face of basic economics, it makes sense when one considers that financial concerns are not the only ones in play:

a. First, at least in relatively specialized academic settings such as this one, **a person's willingness to volunteer is a strong indicator that s/he has a high aptitude for the subject.** If a person outside a student's family is willing to spend hours on end helping the student without being paid, that willingness is a clear sign that the person strongly values and at least moderately enjoys the subject matter. In turn, these traits are usually the product of long-term dedication to the subject – the kind of dedication that begins with natural aptitude, is encouraged by initial success, and feeds the cycle by bringing improvement and the further success and encouragement that accompany it.

b. Second, all else being equal, **such a volunteer's help will be more time-efficient – *i.e.*, more effective per unit of time that s/he and the student jointly invest – than will the help of a paid tutor.** A tutor whose reward comes from the work itself will have both *a*) the incentive to do a good and thorough job and *b*) the incentive *not* to waste one's own time or that of one's partner (here, the student) in the process. Instead, a volunteer has the incentive to complete a given task with diligence and without undue delay, moving on to either the next task in the project (here, helping the student with another exercise) or something else that the volunteer needs to do.

By contrast, the financial interests of a paid tutor are often not aligned with the student's interests and indeed may conflict with them: Paying a tutor by the hour removes the incentive toward time efficiency and, if work hours are not fixed, even *creates* an incentive toward *inefficiency*. The alternative is little better: Paying by the task (if one can even divide work of this type into discrete tasks) encourages a tutor to rush through lessons and to pay insufficient attention both to instructional quality and to whether the student comprehends the material.

Students who live near large numbers of college students, talented high schoolers, professional tutors, and other potential "employees" are fortunate that tutors in their area have a lower-than-average likelihood of abusing these incentives: As the number of potential tutors increases, so does their need to compete against each other for part-time work (in the case of older students) or clientele (in the case of tutors), and so will the level of diligence that they must exhibit if they are to hold on to their jobs.

In addition, **if a student already faces unreasonably high expectations and/or pressure from his or her parents (or comparable authority figures), the quantifiable expense of a paid tutor can make matters even worse.**

- Parents of this type, who are rare but not rare enough, are likely to draw the mistaken conclusion that their having spent some specific amount of money entitles them to demand from the student the *quid pro quo* of advancing to some specific level and/or achieving some specific rank. The worst of them may even voice these demands to their child as one more way of ramping up the pressure to attain what they consider success.[23]

- Nor are tutors themselves necessarily above the fray: A parent having the above mindset may place on a tutor demands and pressure similar to those that the parent places on the student. In turn, especially if the parent and the tutor were friends or neighbors before, the desire to avoid disappointing the parent and to maintain good relations in the meantime may give the tutor his or her own motive to increase pressure on the student. Likewise, if the tutor's "day job" involves academic coaching, and especially if the student is among the tutor's everyday clients, the more general desire to maintain or build one's professional reputation may lead the tutor to either consciously or unconsciously place undue pressure on the student.

Of course, it is inevitable that the families of some contestants – perhaps including some families who read and disregard my advice – will seek out and hire spelling-specific coaches despite

---

[23] If any readers worry that by mentioning this tactic I have inadvertently placed it in the mind of one or more "stage parents," I remind those readers that any parent unscrupulous enough to use this tactic would eventually think of it anyway and has likely thought of it already.

having access to the above likely-better alternatives. In practical terms, one is relatively unlikely to encounter such contestants other than at the national competition and the regional competitions of a few highly competitive sponsorship areas, but wherever you yourself notice them, **do not let them intimidate you.**

- If during your preparations for competition a run-in with a professionally coached contestant makes you feel less likely to succeed, do not let the perceived change in odds and incentives tempt you to reduce or abandon your efforts. Doing so will only bring reality in line with your perceptions.

- If just before competition or during a break you see a contestant and coach doing rapid-fire drills while perched conspicuously in a lobby or at a table, the odds are good that they are putting on a tightly scripted show as if it were a substantive display of skill, and you should see through and dismiss their attempt to "rattle" the competition.

Instead, return your focus to where it belongs: before competition, on your own preparatory efforts (redoubled in light of your greater awareness of your needs); and during competition, on your knowledge and thought processes (including, when necessary, the stress-management techniques that you have developed).

Regardless of the context, remember to maintain proper perspective:

- At least within the bounds of sportsmanlike conduct, your performance is the only one that you can control.

- Your performance is the only one that determines whether you advance to the next round.

- Finally, **if you take full advantage of the resources that already surround you, your chances of survival are better than your rivals would have you think.**

FINAL THOUGHTS:
CHANCE AND LUCK[24]

Perhaps the most frequent criticism of spelling bee competition is that it's "all a matter of luck" – that a competitor's success or failure depends merely on what word the competitor receives in a given round, with the effect that if that competitor had received someone else's word from that round, he or she might have advanced or been eliminated rather than vice versa.

This criticism is mostly misplaced for one crucial reason: As far as preparation and competition are concerned, very little of the chance affecting your success in spelling bees can be accurately described as luck. **Luck is chance over which one has no control, and you have a significant amount of control over your chances in competition.** Competitive spelling may be thought of as a game of skill and preparation, a game of chance, or both, but **in a spelling bee, most chance is reducible to the skill and preparation that determine it.**

Your percent chance of spelling a randomly selected word is equal to the fraction of words in the dictionary (or, more realistically, of words suitable for use in competition) that you can spell. In other words, it's equal to the fraction of words you have memorized and/or whose patterns you can recognize and apply.

---

[24] Disclosure: Although many of the remarks in this section are similar to some appearing in some versions of the Wikipedia.org article on the Scripps National Spelling Bee, I was the user-editor who first added the text expressing them. The current article, which has been substantially altered since I added my remarks, may be viewed online at http://en.wikipedia.org/wiki/Scripps%20National%20Spelling%20Bee. For my initial and lengthiest contribution on these points and for the absence of discussion of them prior to my contribution, see http://en.wikipedia.org/w/index.php?title=Scripps%20National%20Spelling%20Bee&diff=prev&oldid=74650000.

Equally prepared spellers have an equal *ex ante*[25] chance of correctly spelling a randomly chosen word, even if the particular words that they can spell are different. When you don't know what word you're going to get, the way to improve your chances is to keep studying words, both by memorizing them and by learning the patterns that they follow.

Of course, this scenario is an oversimplification of what happens in competition. Bee officials don't select words for a given round at random. Rather, they look at the set of possible ways in which their pool of words could be assigned – the set of possible *ex post* outcomes – and try to make them as equitable as possible. They do so by trying to choose for each round words of the same objective or intersubjective difficulty (roughly, words that the same fraction of the general population can spell correctly).

They follow this practice because a given word's objective/intersubjective difficulty correlates to some degree with its subjective difficulty for a speller: The less likely the average person is to spell a word correctly, the lower is the *ex ante* chance that the word will fall within the set of words that a given competitor with a given level of preparation and experience can spell. (Of course, the more prepared and seasoned a given competitor is, the smaller the reduction in likelihood will be.)[26]

---

[25] "*Ex ante*" means roughly "[evaluated] from before [an event]," that is, viewed from the perspective of a person who knows what outcomes could happen but doesn't know which one will happen or be revealed. (For example, if you shuffle a deck of standard playing cards and deal one face down, you've already determined what card it is, but the *ex ante* chances that it's an ace – the chances as viewed by you and anyone else at the table – are still one in thirteen or "twelve to one against.")

[26] Because both a word's objective/intersubjective difficulty and a speller's level of individual preparation affect that speller's *ex ante* likelihood of correctly spelling that word, estimating that likelihood is

To the extent that officials succeed in selecting words of equal objective difficulty for a round, equally prepared competitors have equal *ex ante* chances of advancing, and the competition is fair despite any inequality of outcome. To the extent that deliberately selected words are of different objective difficulty, however, luck enters the picture. If you get an objectively easier or harder word than does the person next to you and if the two of you are equally prepared, then you will have different chances of advancing.

In my observation, this effect is especially pronounced in the middle rounds of national competition. Although words given during these rounds often have similar etymologies (for example, being derived directly from Latin or Greek) and therefore follow similar phonetic patterns, some are more frequently seen in print than others. For this reason, it's possible for any two spellers to get a pair of words for which *a)* neither speller could figure out or sound out either word and *b)* both spellers have seen one word in print but *c)* neither speller has seen the other word in print.

By the end of national competition, however, every word is seldom seen in print, is hard to sound out, and can be figured out only by the small number of people who have the skills to have advanced that far. (These spellers would have known or figured out their words in early and middle rounds whether those words were commonly seen in print or not, so luck likely wouldn't have helped them during the rounds in which it could have made a difference.) Thus, at the end of competition, objective difficulty is so high for all words that it is a non-issue

---

quite difficult if one does not know what languages and source materials the speller has studied. Although I am not an expert in statistics, my guess is that in the absence of this type of background information, one would have to first measure the speller's ability as a percentile ranking in the general population and then find out what percentage of the people at that percentile rank can spell that word.

as between any of them, and preparation is virtually all that matters.

For these reasons, **as between well-prepared spellers, the primary role of luck is to affect spellers' placement within the middle ranks of national competition.** As of this writing, advancement or elimination a few rounds earlier or later makes a difference in prize money of a few hundred dollars one way or the other. Luck has an effect, but that effect is nowhere nearly as significant as critics like to claim.

Indeed, *ex ante* equality would permit some undeserved inequality of outcome even if bee officials adopted many critics' suggestion and conducted the bee as a series of written rounds in which each contestant received the same word. Just as a speller in traditional competition does not know what word he or she will receive, no speller under this format would know what word the spellers would receive. Either way, therefore, two spellers prepared to the same degree would stand the same *ex ante* chance that their word falls within the set of words they can spell. Thus, they would be subject to the same odds as in a traditional competition, assuming all words in a round are of equal objective difficulty. Because it would still be a matter of chance whether each round's word is within the set of words for which a contestant is prepared, equally prepared contestants still might end up on opposite sides of the odds in a given round.

For related reasons, an inequality familiar to participants in traditional competition could still occur over the course of a bee: A contestant could know words given early in competition and advance through early rounds despite not knowing words given later even as a contestant equally prepared (and with equal *ex ante* chances) knew words given later but, having been unfamiliar with words given early on, might not last to spell them.

104

Undeserved inequality of outcome could be reduced somewhat by changing the "miss-and-out" structure to one in which each contestant spells the same number of words and the contestant giving the most correct spellings is declared the winner. Yet even under this system – and even if officials went so far as to sequester the contestants and give each of them the same *set* of words – the initial selection of words to use in competition could create inequality of outcome between spellers familiar with an equal fraction of the set of words suitable for competition.

Moreover, each of these changes would either undermine the academic benefits of preparation or make competition prohibitively time-consuming:

- Spellers taking a written test at the same time, whether round by round or for an overall score, cannot draw on their preparation by asking questions about words' specific roots. A written test therefore favors contestants who rely on rote memorization at the expense of contestants who study a broader range of materials and use pattern recognition and analogy. In the process, it creates a disincentive to use more advanced reasoning skills and reduces the educational value of competitive spelling.

- If a competition's officials were to both *a*) proceed speller by speller (in order to preserve spellers' ability to ask questions) and *b*) allow all spellers to remain in the competition until its end, that competition would take an inordinately long time.

Having each contestant spell an identical set of words out of earshot of other contestants, such that each contestant would receive the same words but could ask his or her own questions, would make matters even worse: Reducing a bee's word list to two or three dozen words (at the very most) would make the contest far less informative – and, albeit less importantly, far less exciting – for its spectators.

For these reasons, the only way to completely remove luck from the competition would be to reduce the competition to an absurdity: to have contestants spell every word in the dictionary for an overall score. In turn, the only way to do so while still allowing them to ask questions about specific roots would be even more absurd: to go through the entire dictionary with each contestant one at a time in a soundproof room. Of course, such a procedure is possible only in theory, and anything even remotely resembling it would make the competition take so much time that its participants would learn more by doing something else.

Because the question-and-answer process necessitates that spellers compete one at a time and because word selection and "miss-and-out" elimination are necessary to keep speller-by-speller competition from being time-prohibitive, **the traditional spelling bee format, despite its potential for undeserved inequality of outcome, is the best way to keep competitive spelling both true to its educational mission and practically feasible.**

Looking at the "big picture," however, **the critics do have a point: Long before you begin preparing for your first bee, luck plays a major role in your chances for success in competitive spelling – the same role that it plays in your chances for success in life – and the farther you advance, the better you would do to let that fact lend perspective to even your most justified sense of accomplishment.**

To a significant degree, both your raw aptitude for the study of languages and your opportunities to make the most of that aptitude are determined by circumstances beyond your control. The most notable form of this luck is the "parental lottery," the accidents of birth that inspire the saying "you can't pick your parents": Various studies suggest that inherited traits account for about 40% to 60% of the degree to which a person's intelligence is above or below average.[27] On top of that, your parents' wealth and the number of your siblings affect your access to childhood nutrition, critical for neurological development. These factors, your parents' employment commitments, and their love for you affect their ability and willingness to invest time and resources in you (for example, by reading to you), shaping your intellectual development prior to school age. Your parents' wealth and their choice of where to live determine your access to primary and secondary educational institutions, and their willingness to assist with your classwork and extracurricular activities affects how much you benefit from whatever institution you attend. Finally, if you were born in the United States, you are lucky to have gotten your start in a country whose political system allows intellectual freedom and academic institutions – of which competitive spelling is but one – to flourish, at least for now.

This last point is related to the most fundamental luck of all, at least as far as school-age competitors are concerned: The only people who can win spelling bees are people lucky enough to live where competitive spelling exists. If you have this first bit of luck, then regardless of whether your other circumstances make a top finish possible, you can use competitive spelling to have fun and develop intellectual abilities that will help you in all areas of life. If these are your ultimate goals, then **spelling bee competition is an effective and rewarding way for you to make the most of whatever luck you have been given.**

---

[27] *See*, for example, Robert Plomin, *Genetics of Childhood Disorders*, JOURNAL OF THE AMERICAN ACADEMY OF CHILD AND ADOLESCENT PSYCHIATRY, volume 38:6, page 786, chapter 3, archived from the Yale University School of Medicine website at http://web.archive.org/web/20060907062252/http://www.med.yale.edu/chldstdy/plomdevelop/genetics/99jungen.htm.

APPENDIX A:
SUGGESTED READING AND VIEWING

The following books and other resources will be useful in your preparation for spelling bee competition, though they are by no means the only materials that you should consult. I receive no royalties, commissions, or other compensation from the sale of any of these materials, even those in which I am featured.

Essentials:

1. The newest book in the *Webster's New International Dictionary* series published as of this writing by Merriam-Webster, Inc. (As of this writing, the latest version is *Webster's Third New International Dictionary*. I recommend the CD-ROM version for reasons that I discuss on page 77–78.)

2. Archived materials from *Carolyn's Corner*, the SNSB-produced but now-defunct online study guide that remains available via the Internet Archive: To visit a webpage listed below, first copy and paste the URL http://web.archive.org/web/20091231235959/ into your browser and then copy and paste the page's URL immediately after it.

    - http://www.spellingbee.com/studyaids.shtml
    - http://www.spellingbee.com/glance.shtml (list of links to advice about specific aspects of competition and preparation)
        - http://www.spellingbee.com/glance/snapshot.shtml (list of spelling "rules"/patterns, organized by language and accompanied by specific examples)
        - http://www.spellingbee.com/glance/organized.shtml (advice about preparing your "spelling notebook")

- Weekly installments featuring study activities and discussions of etymological patterns: http://spellingbee.com/cc[two-digit year number: 97 through 09]/week[two-digit week number]/cchome. htm (for 1997-1999) or /cchome.shtml (for 2000-2009), omitting brackets: Fully accessible weeks are 1 through 17 for 1997, 36 for 1998, 13 for 1999, 23 for 2000, 33 for 2001, 27 for 2002, 32 for 2003, 31 for 2004, 33 for 2005, 34 for 2006, 18 for 2007, 22 for 2008, and 07 for 2009; some subsequent weeks' archives contain some accessible content.

3. *Spell It!*, the SNSB's official list of "study words" for preliminary competition, published online in conjunction with Merriam-Webster, Inc., and available free of charge at http://www.myspellit.com (not to be confused with http://www.spellit.com, an advertiser-owned URL)

   - The authors of *Spell It!* have arranged its words by languages of origin and have included exercises at the end of each section.

   - Note that while the SNSB recommends that local bees use *Spell It!* as their source for competition words, local bees are not bound by this recommendation. They may look elsewhere for words, particularly toward the end of competition when more difficult words are appropriate.

SNSB-developed word lists:

1. The Internet Archive's stored versions of the SNSB's 2003 and 2004 Consolidated Word Lists (CWLs), downloadable from the Internet Archive at http://wayback.archive.org/web/*/http://spellingbee.com /2003* (for 2003's list) and /2004* (for 2004's): See note 12 above for further instructions about downloading these documents.

- The CWL does not provide definitions, word origins, or sentences for all the words that it contains. Be sure to look up definitions and word origins that are not provided.

2. Old Sponsor Bee Guides

3. Old national word lists (either published by the SNSB or compiled from the SNSB's online records)

4. Old SNSB study booklets (*Words of the Champions*, *Paideia*, and *Spell It!*)

- These booklets do not provide definitions along with their words (although *Spell It!* does feature links to dictionary definitions on the Merrriam-Webster official website). Be sure to look up Merriam-Webster's official definitions as you study.

Commercially prepared word lists:

1. The newest edition of Hexco Academic's *Nat's Notes* (published without ISBN): As of September 6, 2014, when this version of this guide (first edition, tenth printing) went to press, the edition released in mid-2012 and titled *New Nat's Notes* is most recent; the previous (February 2007) edition also bears the *New Nat's Notes* title.

- *New Nat's Notes* and other Hexco products are available for purchase online at http://www.hexco.com.

Dictionaries of technical terminology (be sure to check specific words against Webster's Third*):*

1. Clayton L. Thomas (editor), *Taber's Medical Word Book with Pronunciations*, Philadelphia: F. A. Davis & Co., 1990, ISBN-13 #978-0-8036-8265-9.

2. Bryan A. Garner (editor), *Black's Law Dictionary* (eighth edition), St. Paul, Minn.: West Group, 2004, ISBN-13 #978-0-3141-5199-0. (Check all spellings in this work against *Webster's Third*. Also, because this work is expensive, look for a used copy — if you live near a law school, the law school or campus bookstore is a good place to look.)

Newspapers and other periodicals:

1. The newspaper or other publication that sponsors your regional competition

2. *The Economist* (Watch out for British spellings!)

Other guidebooks for spelling bee preparation and competition:

1. Barrie Trinkle, Carolyn Andrews, and Paige Kimble, *How to Spell Like a Champ: Roots, Lists, Rules, Games, Tricks, & Bee-Winning Tips from the Pros*, New York: Workman Publishing, 2006, ISBN-13 #978-0-7611-4369-7. (Disclosure: I am acknowledged on page viii and quoted on pages 44 and 160 of this book.)

Insightful examinations of the spelling bee "experience":

1. James Maguire, *American Bee: The National Spelling Bee and the Culture of Word Nerds*, Emmaeus, Pa.: Rodale Books, 2006, ISBN-13 #978-1-5948-6214-4. (Disclosure: I am profiled on pages 111 through 114 of this book.)

2. Jeffrey Blitz (director), *Spellbound* (film), 2002, ISBN-10 #1-4049-4760-4, ISBN-13 #978-1-4049-4760-3. (Disclosure: In this documentary I have two brief, uncredited appearances as an SNSB staff member leading contestants off stage after they misspell. One of those contestants is

documentary subject Emily Stagg; the other, not identified in the film, is shown taking an elaborate bow.)

APPENDIX B:
QUICK REFERENCE

Suggested organization of "spelling notebook" (summary):

I. Master list sorted by language of origin

    A. Language (one division for each language)

        1. List of spelling rules and patterns governing this language

        2. Alphabetized list of this language's specific roots and their meanings (one subdivision for each root)

            a) Alphabetized list of word entries involving a given root (one entry per word)

                (1) Word to be studied

                (2) Definition(s) of word

                (3) Etymology of word

II. Same master list sorted by subject matter

    A. List of spelling rules and patterns for the various languages whose words appear on your list

        1. Language-specific list of rules and patterns (one list per language)

    B. Subject matter (one division for each subject)

        1. Language of origin (one division for each language)

            a) Alphabetized list of this language's specific roots and their meanings (one subdivision for each root found in one or more words related to this subject)

                (1) Alphabetized list of word entries involving a given root (one entry per word)

                    (a) Word to be studied

                    (b) Definition(s) of word

                    (c) Etymology of word

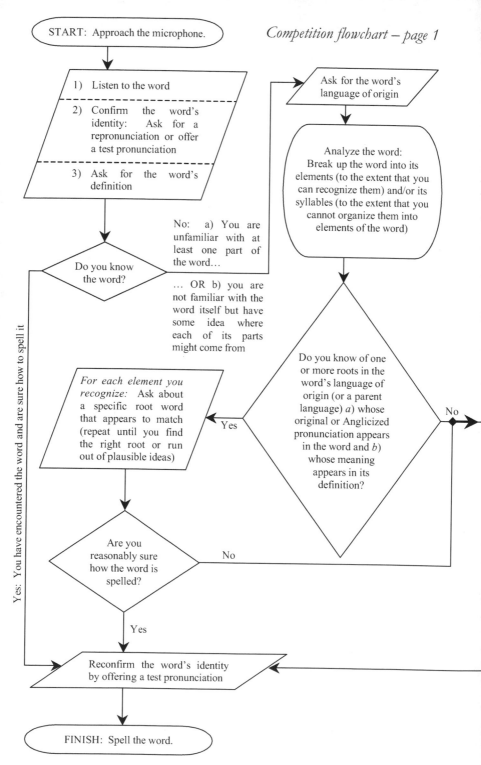

START: Approach the microphone.

Competition flowchart – page 1

1) Listen to the word

2) Confirm the word's identity: Ask for a repronunciation or offer a test pronunciation

3) Ask for the word's definition

Ask for the word's language of origin

Analyze the word: Break up the word into its elements (to the extent that you can recognize them) and/or its syllables (to the extent that you cannot organize them into elements of the word)

Do you know the word?

No: a) You are unfamiliar with at least one part of the word…

… OR b) you are not familiar with the word itself but have some idea where each of its parts might come from

For each element you recognize: Ask about a specific root word that appears to match (repeat until you find the right root or run out of plausible ideas)

Do you know of one or more roots in the word's language of origin (or a parent language) *a)* whose original or Anglicized pronunciation appears in the word and *b)* whose meaning appears in its definition?

Yes

No

Yes: You have encountered the word and are sure how to spell it

Are you reasonably sure how the word is spelled?

No

Yes

Reconfirm the word's identity by offering a test pronunciation

FINISH: Spell the word.

114

"For emergency use only":
Ask these questions only if you're genuinely stuck.
Otherwise, save your time and the judges' patience
for when you really need them.

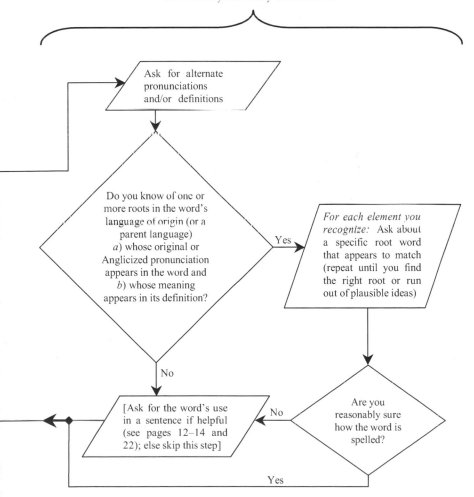

Ask for alternate pronunciations and/or definitions

Do you know of one or more roots in the word's language of origin (or a parent language)
a) whose original or Anglicized pronunciation appears in the word and
b) whose meaning appears in its definition?

For each element you recognize: Ask about a specific root word that appears to match (repeat until you find the right root or run out of plausible ideas)

Yes

No

[Ask for the word's use in a sentence if helpful (see pages 12–14 and 22); else skip this step]

No

Are you reasonably sure how the word is spelled?

Yes

NOTES

40824012R00073

Made in the USA
Middletown, DE
24 February 2017